I Will Lift Up Mine Eyes

Psalm 121:1

LINDA GANDY

PAGE PUBLISHING
Conneaut Lake, PA

First originally published by Page Publishing 2023

ISBN 978-1-6624-7193-3 (pbk)
ISBN 978-1-6624-7194-0 (digital)

Printed in the United States of America

Acknowledgement

In apperception in preparing this book, there has been several people that assisted me. I am deeply grateful to them. They are my children Dawn, Brian, and Susan. Also to Pam Harris and Candace Riner (who were a tremendous help), Ronda Lambert, and Katie Patterson. These ladies always had a smile and exercised great patience with me. Most of all, I am thankful to the Lord for giving me this opportunity and seeing me through all the adventures.

The Friendship Bowl

Polly Attwood was making a last-minute check over every inch of the house before their dinner guests arrived. Going from room to room, she found herself wondering again about all the earlier Attwood wives who had taken care of their families in this very house since the first Attwoods homesteaded the property over 150 years ago. Every room, adorned with treasured family heirlooms, gave Polly the feeling that a lot of love had been in this house, giving each generation a solid foundation of security. Satisfied that everything was in order, she went into the dining room.

Walking over to the china cabinet, Polly smiled as she removed the *Friendship Bowl*—a vegetable bowl, oval in shape, with scalloped-fluted edges. The ivory background accented the tiny blue blossoms and sprigs of green. The bowl had once belonged to Polly's great-grandmother, and each time the bowl was handed down from Mother to daughter, the instructions were the same—use it, enjoy it, do not sit it on a shelf just to look at.

As Polly was removing other serving dishes from the cabinet, she heard her husband, Tom, come in the back door. Polly carefully carried the stack of dishes into the kitchen where she saw Tom standing by the stove, fork in hand, sampling a chunk of meat. He looked like a little boy with his hand caught in the cookie jar.

Polly shook her finger at him and was about to deliver a wifely scolding when Tom spoke up, "Polly-girl, this roast is almost done. Sure is juicy and tender." He took a sideways glance at Polly and continued, "You know, it is a wonder that I don't tip the scales at three hundred pounds after all these years of eating your good cooking."

Polly's hand dropped to her side, and she laughed outright. "Tom Attwood, that is the third sample of roast you've had. I'm

1

beginning to wonder if there will be enough for our guests, Bro. and Mrs. Rutledge. Oh, I almost forgot, they asked us to call them Henry and Ellen. They will be here in fifteen minutes, and they are going to catch you in your dirty work clothes if you don't go upstairs and get ready. Be sure you put those dirty clothes in the hamper, and don't leave the bathroom in a mess."

"Gee, Polly, they won't be going upstairs."

Polly turned to resume her finishing touches for the meal when suddenly she could not move. Tom had walked up behind her and engulfed her in a big bear hug. Leaning his head to one side, he kissed her on the cheek. Polly relaxed and leaned against him. Her whole world was right here. She thought again about how lucky she was. Tom was a man of his word, and the folks in the community valued his friendship. The faith he had in his heavenly Father was rock solid.

Polly stood there, and for a moment, her thoughts drifted back to a time years ago when they were expecting their first child. Dr. Post, their family doctor and longtime friend, informed them that they had better buy two of everything because twins were coming to their house. In a flurry of joy and surprise, Tom and Polly transformed a spare bedroom into a fully equipped nursery for two.

Finally after the long months of waiting, Tom drove Polly to the hospital and eagerly awaited the arrival of the twins, but something went terribly wrong. Polly barely survived, the twins did not. Before Tom and Polly could even grasp what had happened, there were two tiny graves in the family plot of the age-old cemetery adjoining the church where Tom and Polly had faithfully attended for years. They both thought that losing the twins was the worst thing that could happen until a few days later, Dr. Post came into Polly's hospital room, took her hand, and in his gentle way, told them that Polly could never have any more children.

During the difficult days that followed, Tom and Polly were a comfort to each other, but Tom's faith was so strong that there were times that Polly felt resentment and envy. But that was forty years ago, and though it did not come easy, Polly developed her own strong faith. With a deep sigh, Polly brought her thoughts back to the present. She turned to Tom.

"I am so glad Henry and Ellen have come our way. I believe he is just the pastor our church needs, even though he is young and has had little experience pastoring a church. I feel that he is going to seek you out often for advice and counsel. He won't regret it. You will be wise and objective."

"Dear lady, on that good note, I will take my leave."

Polly stood there in the middle of the kitchen floor, hands on hips, and a twinkle in her eyes. She called after him as he started upstairs, "Remember what I said about the bathroom."

Smiling to herself, she checked the roast, not that there was any need. She lifted other lids and gave a stir here and there.

From her garden were golden-brown potatoes and glazed carrots cooked with the roast, seasoned green beans simmering long and slow, and fruit salad folded into thick whipped cream. To complement the meal, there would be piping-hot corn bread and gravy, crisp, sweet pickles, and iced tea. Their own trees provided the peaches for the cobbler, juicy and bubbling beneath a flaky lattice topped crust. Homemade vanilla ice cream was ready to go on top. Polly ground the coffee beans and made the coffee. While setting four cups and saucers on the table, she heard the doorbell ring. Removing her apron and smoothing her hair, she started down the hall. As she passed the foot of the stairs, she paused. Tom was coming down the stairs, buttoning a sleeve cuff on the way.

In an undertone, Polly asked, "What does the bathroom look like?"

Tom grinned and winked. "You would never know I was there."

As they approached the front door, Polly enjoyed a good look at it. It was one of her favorite features of the house. It was of solid oak with an oval glass inset that extended about the full length of the door. Part of the glass was a frosted scene of gently rolling hills covered with lovely flowers. It looked much like the view from any window of the house.

Tom opened the door, and with a welcoming smile, he and Polly greeted their guests. After a brief conversation, Polly led the way to the dining room. With everyone in place around the table, Tom asked that they join hands for the blessing.

3

LINDA GANDY

Tom prayed, "Dear Father, thank You for this day and the strength to do our daily tasks. We especially thank You for sending Henry and Ellen our way. May our church family daily seek your will. Guide our new pastor as he leads us. Now, Father, I ask your blessing on the one that prepared this meal. I ask this prayer in Jesus' name. Amen."

Three other amens resounded around the table.

Polly began passing the food, and as she picked up the *friendship bowl*, Ellen exclaimed, "Polly! My set of china is the exact pattern as this bowl. I have never seen this pattern anywhere else until now."

Polly replied, "I think it is a pretty bowl, and I do enjoy using it mostly because it belonged to my great-grandmother."

The meal progressed with a steady interchange of conversation. Tom had a look of complete bliss as he took another helping of cornbread and gravy.

Polly smothered a chuckle and thought, *Those predinner samples didn't faze his appetite one bit.*

When everyone was beyond eating another bite, Polly suggested having coffee on the front porch.

Henry and Ellen noticed that the wide porch had a comfortable and inviting look. Ceiling fans softly hummed, stirring the pleasant night air. The wide porch railing made an attractive setting for Polly's many potted plants. The chairs had thick, soft, padded cushions, but the swing was the conversation piece. The backrest was made so that it could be reversed from one side of the swing to the other. This way, when Tom and Polly used the swing, they could choose which way they wanted to look while swinging. Often on summer nights, as Tom and Polly relaxed on the porch, friends or neighbors would happen by and stop for a visit.

As the four sat down, Tom remarked about the full moon just clearing the treetops. It looked like a giant orange pumpkin, casting a mellow light over the yard and adjoining fields. The only sounds were the songs of the katydids and whip-poor-wills.

Henry took a deep breath and asked, "Tom, how in the world do you keep things caught up around the place with this peaceful porch tempting you?"

4

Tom laughed. "I'll tell you, Henry, there are times that I don't even consider what I need to be doing. I just come out here, sit down for a few minutes, and enjoy God's beautiful handiwork."

Henry nodded his head. "I can certainly understand that. Say, Tom, didn't I hear something the other day about the men having a paint day at the church tomorrow?"

"Yes, you did. We wanted to have it all done before you got here, but the weather didn't cooperate."

"I sure would like to help. During my college summers, I worked for my uncle, who was a carpenter by trade. It would feel good to have a paintbrush in my hands again. Besides, it would give me an opportunity to get better acquainted with the men."

"Henry, you are welcome to come, and I'll be glad to bring an extra paintbrush. We plan to get started at eight o'clock and be finished by noon."

The evening passed quickly, and before they realized it, the moon was high in the sky. Henry and Ellen expressed their thanks for a delightful evening with Henry adding that he especially enjoyed the delicious peach cobbler. Then they said their goodbyes.

Sometime later, with the dishes done and everything in order, Tom and Polly went upstairs to bed. Before long, Polly heard Tom's even breathing and knew that he was sound asleep. Polly laid there wide awake thinking of the little bits and pieces of conversation that brought questions to her mind.

It was probably just her imagination, but what if? She quietly got out of bed and went to the spare bedroom. Turning on a lamp, she raised the lid of a camelback trunk and removed a stack of yellowed papers, tied together with a faded ribbon. Sitting in a rocking chair and leaning slightly toward the lamplight, she began to read from her great-grandmother Jane's journal. Polly had read it many times, but tonight, she would pay special attention to every detail. Hopefully she would find answers to some of the questions on her mind. As she read on, some loose ends seem to fit together, but there were questions that remained unanswered. Those would have to wait until tomorrow, so she turned out the lamp and quietly returned to bed.

The next morning, Polly awoke with a start and looked at the clock. Bright sunlight was streaming through the windows, and she could hear Tom in the bathroom getting dressed. She bounded out of bed, grabbed her robe, and flew down the stairs.

In minutes, the bacon was sizzling, and the coffee was brewing. Polly scrambled the eggs as Tom came into the kitchen, whistling as he sat down at the table. She dished up their breakfast, and they discussed their plans for the day. Polly told Tom that she thought that she would stop by the parsonage to talk to Ellen, but she would be back in time to fix lunch. She reminded him about the extra paintbrush.

As Polly drove to the parsonage, she thought again of the questions that kept coming to her mind the night before. A short time later, Polly was turning into the driveway of the parsonage.

Ellen waved to her as she finished watering her flowers. "My, you are lively today, especially after preparing that delicious feast for us last night. Let's go in, and I'll make us a glass of iced tea."

Polly said, "Didn't we have a good time though?"

Ellen motioned for Polly to take a seat in the living room, but as Polly walked to her seat, she saw a picture on the a table and went over to it instead, saying, "Ellen, tell me about this picture."

Ellen picked up the picture and studied it for a moment. "The lady on our left is my great-grandmother, Maria. In fact, the set of china that I mentioned to you last night was hers originally, but that is about all I know. I do not know who the lady is that is standing next to her, although I have often wondered about her. Aren't they pretty? Just look at those high collars and full skirts. Did you ever see so much material in one dress? I wonder if they were on their way to some special event?"

Polly could not keep the excitement out of her voice. "Ellen, did your great-grandmother come from Austria?"

Ellen looked surprised and puzzled. "Why yes, she, or rather, they did. Kurt and Maria Zweig were my great-grandparents, but how in the world would you know this?"

Polly's eyes were sparkling. "Ellen, let's sit down because I have a story that you will find both interesting and exciting."

Ellen motioned toward the couch, and as the two ladies sat down, Ellen turned to Polly. "You certainly have aroused my curiosity. I'm eager to hear your story."

Polly took a deep breath and began.

*****

In 1895, a couple, Kurt and Maria Zweig, left Austria to come to America. They settled in Oakdale, New York. On the day of their arrival, a neighbor lady knocked on their door with a basket on her arm. A pretty lady in house cleaning clothes opened the door. She had a cloth covering her hair to protect it from all the dust, but a few unruly curls had escaped, framing a smiling face. The neighbor lady said, "Hello, I'm Jane Nelson, and I live just across the street with my husband, John. I just came over to welcome you to our neighborhood."

Maria wiped her hands on her apron. "I am Maria Zweig. Please come in. I am afraid things are in a mess right now."

As Jane entered the front room and sat the basket on a table, she replied, "Don't worry about any mess. I remember how it was when John and I moved into our house. I felt sure you would be busy all day unpacking and getting your things in place, so I brought over a loaf of fresh baked bread while it is still warm and some of my strawberry jam to go with it."

Just then, Kurt appeared in the room. "Something smells good."

Maria laughed and reached her hand out to Kurt as she made the introduction.

"My husband got a whiff of your bread, Jane. Always in Austria, when I baked bread, Kurt would be sitting at the table with knife in hand, ready to spread the butter just as soon as the bread was cool enough to slice. Somehow he could always tell the right moment to take a break from work."

Jane took the bread and jam out of the basket and said, "I know John will want to meet both of you, and since you will probably be very tired by tonight, would you come over and have supper with us?"

7

Maria looked at Kurt. He smiled at her and nodded.

Maria took Jane's hand. "Thank you so much. We will be happy to come."

"Good. We eat at six o'clock but come over a little early so both of you can get acquainted with John. I am going to get out of your way now. See you at six."

Later that day, when John returned from work, Jane told him of their new neighbors and the dinner invitation.

The evening was a complete success. The food was delicious, and the two couples talked throughout the meal as though they had always known each other. Later as Kurt and Maria crossed the street to their house, they had a good feeling about their new friends and about America. And tonight, they would sleep in their own bed for the first time since arriving in this country.

The next morning, Jane was just finishing her ironing when Maria appeared at the front door.

"Come in, Maria. I'm almost done and then we can have a cup of tea. I've been thinking for the past ten minutes how good a cup would taste."

Maria noticed the pillowcase Jane was ironing. "That is a lovely edging. What is it called?"

Jane ran the sad iron across the pillowcase for one last time then handed the pillowcase to Maria.

As Jane touched the edging, she said, "It is called the triple-leaf pattern, and I love to crochet it."

Maria studied the design then handed the pillowcase back to Jane. "I would love for you to show me how to make it one of these days. By the way, I meant to ask you last night but I forgot. Will you tell me the names of the stores where you do your shopping?"

Jane poured up their tea then reached for paper and pencil. "I'll jot the names down for you. Let's see, Haverty's for your meats, O'Brien's for fresh produce, and Steinbergs for home furnishings. All the stores are close by too."

Maria looked over the list Jane had given her. "This will save me a lot of time, and speaking of time, I must go. I still have a full day's work ahead of me even with Kurt helping all day yesterday. Thanks so much for the tea. It was just what I needed."

Over time, the friendship grew between the two couples. On Saturday afternoons, they enjoyed a buggy ride into the country for a picnic lunch. Often, they would get together and make a freezer of ice cream. Then they would gather around the piano and harmonize one song after another while the ice cream ripened.

Then came the day no one anticipated. Kurt was given an opportunity for a promotion with his company, but it meant moving to another city. As much as they loved where they lived and their friendship with John and Jane, they decided to take the promotion. Too soon, moving day was upon them.

Maria had allowed a few minutes to visit with Jane before they left. In Jane's front room, Maria handed her a cloth bundle. As Jane folded back the cloth, she saw a piece from Maria's set of china.

"Jane, you have been a friend from the moment we arrived. Kurt and I value our friendship with you and John. I want you to take this vegetable bowl and use and enjoy it. Don't sit it on a shelf just to look at. Let it be a symbol of our friendship."

Jane said, "Maria, I know how much you treasure your china. I thank you, and I promise that I will use it and often. I will tell the story of our friendship to my children so that when I pass this down to one of them, it will have special meanings of friendship for them as well. Why, Maria, that's just what I will call it, my *Friendship Bowl*. Let's do keep in touch. When you and Kurt get settled in your new place, write to us and include your new address. Now don't go just yet because I have something for you." Jane handed a package wrapped in tissue paper to Maria. In her hands was a pair of snowy-white pillowcases with the triple-leaf crocheted pattern. Jane folded one edge of the hem back to show a small embroidered J. N. "I don't want you to forget me."

Tears rolled down Maria's cheeks as she leaned over and gave Jane a hug. "Oh, Jane, when Kurt and I get moved, you won't be there to bring over a loaf of bread and strawberry jam. How I am going to miss you. But the pillowcases are a lovely reminder of our friendship, and they are special to me."

There was a knock at the door, and Kurt said it was time to go. Jane walked outside with them and stood in the yard, waving until Kurt and Maria were out of sight. With a deep sigh, she walked back into the house.

She thought, *I think that tonight I will prepare one of John's favorite desserts, apple pie. Right now, I am not sure just what else we will have for supper, but I know I will use my friendship bowl.*

Both Jane and Maria lived long happy lives, remaining in touch faithfully until Maria's death severed the connections between the families.

*****

As Polly finished her story, she looked again at the picture that Ellen was still holding. "Well, Ellen, that's the story. I read enough from my great-grandmother Jane's journal last night to be certain of some facts, but I still had some unanswered questions until a moment ago when I saw that picture. You see, I have one just like it. That made all the pieces fit together."

"Polly, what a fantastic story. I feel like I have been time traveling. I almost feel as though I just had a visit with those two ladies."

Polly replied, "I know what you mean. I felt the same way last night as I read in Jane's journal. You know, tying all these loose ends together has solved a problem for me. I have wondered over the years just what I would do with the *Friendship Bowl* when it comes my time to pass it down. Since we have no children, I was at a loss until now. Ellen, I want you to have the bowl. It will be almost like a homecoming, and I know you will treasure it."

Ellen looked at Polly. "I will be honored to have the bowl, but only when you are finished with it. It will be placed along with the rest of my great-grandmother's china, but it will always have a special place in my heart. My goodness, I almost forgot. Come with me." Ellen walked into one of their spare bedrooms, and there on the bed was a pair of pillowcases with a triple-leaf crocheted pattern. Ellen turned back the hem of one case and pointed to the two letters *J* and *N*. "I knew they were there but never knew what they meant until now."

Polly gently ran her fingers along the edging. She could almost see her great-grandmother Jane as she crocheted the triple-leaf edging.

Polly looked at her watch and exclaimed, "Gracious me, I've got to go. I told Tom I would be home by noon. I won't make it if I don't hurry. But what a morning it has been."

Ellen walked Polly to the front door. "I am so glad you have Jane's journal. Just think how the *Friendship Bowl* and pillowcases have come full circle. Come back soon, so we can talk some more."

"Ellen, I look forward to another visit too. I can't help but think how surprised and pleased Jane and Maria would be if they could know where the *Friendship Bowl* and the pillowcases are today, and the way it all came about. But for now, I must go."

As Polly drove home, she thought, *I think tonight, I will make one of Tom's favorite desserts, chocolate pie. I'm not sure what else we will have for supper, but I am going to use my Friendship Bowl.*

A Country Christmas

The year was 1929, and times were hard. The small, rural community of Cherry Hill was quite different then. It had a barbershop, blacksmith shop, cotton gin, gristmill, and two large department stores—much like general stores. There were also two physicians, Dr. Philpot and Dr. Lee.

The members of the Highland Methodist Church were planning their annual Christmas Program. The play entitled "Last Year's Christmas Doll" was taken from the magazine, *The Christian Herald*. All the parts for the play had been assigned. Several men of the church had offered to provide a big, full tree for the program. As usual, the young people were responsible for the decorations for the tree.

Several months earlier, immediately after church one Sunday morning, the young people had gathered under one of the giant oak trees in the church yard to discuss how they might get decorations for the Christmas tree. They knew that none of the families had any extra decorations or money to spare.

One of the group asked, "Why don't we save our pennies? If we each save every penny possible, we might have enough to buy something for decorations."

Another one of the group spoke up, saying, "I agree. Do you all remember when one of the globes of a kerosene lamp at church was broken? Everyone saved pennies until enough money was collected to purchase a new globe. We could save pennies this time, so we could buy decorations."

One of the boys asked, "How much money do you think we would need?"

Someone spoke up and said, "I think if we can save up twenty-five cents, we can purchase decorating supplies."

After some thought, the group decided that each one of them would save every penny they possibly could. Having made their decision, the group scattered to join their families who were already in their wagons, ready to go.

During the following weeks, the young people were mindful of their promise to save pennies. Each one of the group found a container to keep their pennies in. From time to time, they would ask each other how much they had saved up. The total slowly increased. One cent would buy needed things, so it was very difficult for each young person to save even one penny.

The days seemed to fly by quickly. Thanksgiving was coming soon, then it would be Christmastime. The cold air and barren fields were a reminder to all of the young people that they did not have much more time to save their pennies.

After church one Sunday, the group quickly gathered just inside the church door and each one told how much they had saved. The total was fifteen cents. With heavy hearts, they left the church to go home. It looked like they might not get enough to buy anything to make decorations with after all. Well, they were just going to have to try harder.

Finally the time came to count the pennies they had saved. They met at the Ryals' house and each one dumped their pennies out on the kitchen table. Mrs. Ryals counted the small pile of pennies. Everyone held their breath, watching and waiting. At last, they saw Mrs. Ryals' smile as she raised her head.

She said, "There are twenty-five pennies here. Congratulations, you have done a fine job."

What excitement there was in the Ryals' house that afternoon. To celebrate the occasion, Mrs. Ryals made hot chocolate for the young people and served them gingerbread, fresh from the oven. After enjoying the tasty refreshments, the young people left the Ryals' house and walked from there to town, where they entered one of the department stores. They took their time looking around at everything in the store, wanting to be sure the money was spent wisely. After several ideas were discussed, they made their decision. They bought some crepe paper and tinfoil with the total coming to twenty-five cents.

One of the girls in the group lived nearby and invited the young people to come to her house to make the decorations. Soon after they arrived, everyone got busy. Some cut the crepe paper into strips, which were made into a long chain. This chain would be wound around and around the Christmas tree from top to bottom. The other young people cut squares of tinfoil. In each square was placed a sweet gumball with a piece of string attached. Then the foil was crimped around the sweet gumball. These would be hung on the tree. Before long, the decorations were complete and put in a safe place until the time came to decorate the tree.

The young people felt a great relief to know that the Christmas decorations were taken care of. The past few years had not been easy for anyone in the community. Families had done without things they needed and made do with what they had on hand. It would be a little more meaningful this year to enter the church the night of the Christmas Program and know that they had found a way to provide the tree decorations.

At last, the day came for the Christmas Program. Families had worked harder all day to get chores done a little earlier so that everyone would have time to wash up and put on their Sunday best.

Later that evening as wagons began rolling into the churchyard, children excitedly called out to each other, and adults visited as they entered the church. Inside there was a welcoming glow from the light of the kerosene lamps, but the warmth from the woodstove was most inviting, taking the chill out of everyone's bones.

The Christmas Program was performed to perfection. Lorene Ryals, one of the girls attending that church, played the part of the Christmas Doll. In the story, a little girl's doll had lost an arm and a leg. For the program, Lorene wore a dress belonging to her older sister, Lucy. The dress was loose fitting, so when Lorene slipped one of her arms down inside the dress, it did not show. One of Lorene's legs was carefully bent back at the knee and anchored down behind her, hidden under the dress. With only one arm and one leg showing, Lorene looked exactly like Last Year's Christmas Doll.

When it came time for the presents, everyone's attention was focused on the tree. The parents all exclaimed how pretty the tree looked. Along with the crepe paper chain and the tinfoil wrapped sweet gumballs, there was a present on the tree for every boy and girl in attendance that night. The two Sunday School teachers had seen to that. The boys received identical gifts, and the girls received identical gifts. Every boy and girl felt excitement as each one opened their present. They treasured their gifts and expressed their thanks to the Sunday School teachers.

Before anyone realized it, the evening was over, and it was time to go home. Mothers gathered their children and began bundling them up as dads went outside to check on the teams of horses. Last-minute conversation and goodbyes were exchanged as families loaded into their wagons. The children snuggled under the quilts that were in the wagon beds.

That night as families left the church, going in different directions toward their own homes, there was a warm-hearted feeling in all of their hearts. It had been a good evening. They were thankful for the close bond of caring and sincere fellowship that made up the membership of the church family. Most important of all, however, was the joy of the season. Continuing along their way on the quiet country roads, families looked up into the clear, cold night sky and saw bright twinkling stars. They thought of that night so very long ago when one particular star led the wise men and shepherds to where the Christ Child lied in a manger. For that, they were the most thankful.

Visiting with Grandma Mac

I loved to visit with Grandma Mac. She was my maternal great-grandmother. In addition to my grandfather, whom I called Pappaw, my family consisted of my grandmother, whom I called Mammaw, my parents, and myself.

Grandma Mac lived just across the alley from our house. I visited her often, and during the time when I was just a small child, Mother or Mammaw would walk me to Grandma Mac's house. In an hour or so, one of them would come and walk with me back to our house. The time I spent at Grandma Mac's house was always fun.

Grandma Mac was a small-framed person, but it seemed to me that she could do most anything. Often when I was at her house, she would prepare a tea party for us. We usually had some of her home-made cake or cookies with a glass of cold milk. We would sit there and talk about different things. I felt very grown-up.

As a small child, Grandma Mac's kitchen was a place of pure fascination to me. She had an old wood cookstove. She would raise one of the caps and let me watch her as she put another piece of wood inside. I always had to stand back at a safe distance as she added the wood. She told me that the one thing she thought tasted the best cooked on a woodstove was a big pot of pinto beans. But then, she thought everything tasted better when it was cooked on a woodstove. When she baked a cake, she always sang two verses of her favorite hymn. By then, she knew that the oven was the right temperature to bake the cake. Pappaw had tried for years to get Grandma Mac to have a gas stove. He told her about all the convenient features a gas stove had that her woodstove did not have. He offered to take her shopping. She could pick out the gas stove she liked, and he would buy it for her. Every inch of Grandma Mac's small frame was made of steel. She was having nothing to do with a gas stove. The thing might blow up. Over the years, Pappaw continued to talk about the nice new gas stoves available, but she kept the old woodstove until her dying day.

Grandma Mac did not have a refrigerator either. I thought she had something much more interesting, an icebox. It looked like a small metal box with four legs. Often on a hot day, she would chip small pieces off of the block of ice and fix me a drink of cold water. It always tasted better than the ice water at my house. In fact, one day after I returned home from a visit with Grandma Mac, I asked my family if we could get rid of our refrigerator and get an icebox. I was the only one that thought that was a good idea. The refrigerator stayed at our house.

The most interesting thing about Grandma Mac's icebox was when the iceman came to deliver ice. He used a horse-drawn wagon. He sat on a board stretched across the front part of the wagon. He would lay the reins on the board seat as he stepped down on the ground. I marveled that the horse never moved a single step while the iceman was off of the wagon. The man looked toward Grandma Mac's living room window. There in front of her lacy curtains was a cardboard sign with numbers on it. The way Grandma Mac positioned that sign told the iceman how much ice she wanted that day. Once he knew the weight of ice she wanted, he rolled a very heavy tarp toward the back of the wagon. Next came the part I watched very carefully. He picked up a long pair of tongs from the wagon bed. They looked extremely dangerous to me. He placed the tongs over the block of ice and then as he raised up, the sharp fine pointed ends of the tongs bit into the sides of the block of ice. He carried the ice into Grandma Mac's kitchen and placed it in her icebox. Of the many times I watched the iceman carry ice into Grandma Mac's kitchen, I never one time saw the ice slip out of the grip of those tongs. Returning back to the wagon, he rolled the tarp back over the ice, patted the horse, and got back upon his board seat in the wagon. A word or two to the horse and they were on their way to the next delivery. I never tired of watching the iceman make his delivery to Grandma Mac's house.

Pappaw also tried to persuade Grandma Mac to get a refrigerator. Again, he offered to take her shopping. She could pick out the
refrigerator she liked, and he would buy it for her. He told her that a
refrigerator made its own ice, kept food colder than her icebox, and
was bigger. She could keep more food in it, and the food would stay
good longer. His best efforts fell short of his goal. Grandma Mac had
absolutely no intention of having that electric thing in her house.
Lightning might strike the refrigerator and burn the house down.

Grandma Mac enjoyed working in her colorful flower garden.
There was never a weed there.

Often I would ask her if I could water the flowers, and she
always said, "Yes, I will get the small watering bucket and fill it for
you."

The bucket had a long-necked spout, which had a covered end
with tiny holes in it. It fascinated me to see the water stream out of
those small holes.

Before I knew it, Grandma Mac would say, "Honey, that is
enough water on that flower."

I do not think she ever had a dry flower in her garden.

I was glad Grandma Mac kept her old wood cook stove and icebox. I loved to hear the crackle of the wood burning in the stove. It
made her kitchen feel inviting and cozy. The icebox and watching for
the iceman to arrive will always be a fond memory for me. Grandma
Mac enriched my childhood by sharing her time with me and making me feel welcome when I visited with her.

The Feather Bed and a Giant Oak Tree

I loved feather beds because my maternal great-grandparents had one. Their names were John and Jane Neighbors, but I asked for and received permission to call them Aunt Jane and Uncle John. I did this because I had a large extended family, including grandparents, great-grandparents, uncles, and aunts, who lived within a few blocks of our house. As a small child, giving my maternal great-grandparents the title of aunt and uncle simplified things for me. They lived nine blocks from our house. Every day, Mammaw would go to see her parents, Aunt Jane and Uncle John, and visit with them. Often she would ask me if I would like to go with her. I was delighted to go. I must admit that one reason for my delight was their feather bed.

Soon after we arrived at their house, I would ask Aunt Jane if I could made one jump into their feather bed. She would smile and say, "Yes, you may." From their living room, I made a running start, ending up in their bedroom. Just before I ran into the bed frame, I made a leap that landed me right in the middle of their bed. I remember the pure joy of feeling myself sinking deeper and deeper into the feathers. In a moment's time, I was between two high walls of their feather bed. I would lie there for a short time just to enjoy the fun of my adventure.

When I crawled out of the bed, Aunt Jane was always nearby and would ask me, "Was it fun?"

My reply was simply "Yes, it was a lot of fun."

She fluffed the feathers, straightened the bedspread, and then we returned to the living room where Uncle John and Mammaw were visiting. Over a period of a few years, I made many jumps into that feather bed, feeling a sense of delight each time.

Several years later, when I was in junior high school, there would be times that Aunt Jane would telephone our house and ask Mammaw if she or Mother could bring me over to their house. Aunt Jane wanted me to play the pump organ, so she and Uncle John could sing hymns together. Whichever one had taken the telephone call would tell me what Aunt Jane wanted. All I had to do was just go. They had identical hymn books which we used. If Uncle John said, "Let's sing number twenty-eight," then Aunt Jane and I knew that our number twenty-eight would be the same hymn that Uncle John had.

The pump organ was a lovely piece of furniture in addition to being a fine musical instrument. It did not belong to my great-grandparents. It belonged to a friend of theirs who had gone to California for a year. She had wondered what to do about her organ while she was gone. When she asked Uncle John and Aunt Jane if they would take care of the organ for her, they assured her that they would be happy to do so.

The friend said, "The organ needs to be played. Please use it often."

Aunt Jane and Uncle John always had a number of favorite hymns that they especially enjoyed singing. They sat in their rocking chairs, right next to each other. Uncle John would lean over a little toward Aunt Jane as they harmonized each song. I would listen to them as I played the organ. I noticed that they both still had pleasant singing voices. They just needed someone to play the organ for them. However, after several hymns, I had to concentrate on keeping my feet pumping away at those pedals.

Years earlier, Aunt Jane and Uncle John had taught singing classes in the various Baptist churches. Hymnals with shaped notes were used to teach people to sing who did not read music. Each shaped note represented a different tone of music. Their years of teaching singing classes had long since passed, but they still loved to harmonize hymns together.

Another reason I enjoyed going to see Aunt Jane and Uncle John was because of the family stories she would tell me. One of my favorites was when Aunt Jane and Uncle John were rearing their family of seven children. On a warm, muggy late afternoon, Uncle John noticed storm clouds gathering. There was a closeness in the air to indicate that this was not going to be an ordinary storm. The earlier breeze had developed into a strong wind. Things outside were being tossed here and there. The rain began pounding down. Uncle John gathered the family together. He gave each of the older children a job to do while he hitched the horses to the wagon. When they were finished, they were to come quickly to the wagon. In fast order, the older children took care of the livestock and other jobs they had been assigned to do. Then they rushed to join their mother and the younger children at the wagon. Uncle John helped them into the wagon, cautioning them to sit down and be still. He rushed the horses to a fast pace, knowing that there were two creeks they would have to cross to get to a place of safety. If the rain kept up at the rate it was pouring down now, he questioned whether they would be able to cross the streams. Those streams always rose quickly in a rain like this one. The family held onto the sides of the wagon; concern showing on each face. As the sky grew dark with black clouds, Uncle John felt a knot tighten in his stomach. He knew now that this was not just a bad storm. The roar in the wind told him that there was a tornado not far away. He kept this thought to himself as he did his best to keep the horses going at a steady gait, but it was difficult. The horses sensed that there was trouble.

Aunt Jane kept one eye on the stormy sky as she held the youngest child close on her lap. She did not have to tell the older children to watch over the younger ones. Each of the older children had already put their arms around a younger sister or brother. The storm seemed to get worse every minute. The wind was howling so that it was difficult to speak or be heard. Uncle John urged the horses on.

Finally they arrived at the creek. It was up some, but Uncle John felt sure they could get across. It was a struggle in a place or two, but after what seemed like a long time, the horses pulled the wagon onto solid ground on the other side of the stream. Everyone let out a sigh of relief. Uncle John did his best to keep the horses under control. The horses seemed to sense that the tornado was getting closer.

times get caught in the branches of the trees. Everyone clutched tightly to the tree limbs and wondered if their strength would outlast the storm's fury.

Darkness came. That made everything worse. They could only rely on their ears now to guess what was going on. It had not been all that long since they had left their house, but it seemed like forever. They had a feeling that it was going to be a long night.

Finally the wind became calm, and the rain eased up to a sprinkle. Slowly, Uncle John worked his way from one tree limb to the other, easing around his family as they continued to hold on to the tree limbs.

He jumped to the ground then said, "Jane, help Cora down first. I'll be right here to lift her out of the tree."

Once Cora was on the ground, Uncle John did what he could for her arm. Then one by one, the children eased their way to the bottom limb of the tree, where their father carefully took hold of them and helped them to the ground. When everyone was safely down, Uncle John told them to stay together while he searched for the horses and wagon.

He walked a short distance, and there they were. The horses were still hitched to the wagon. He ran his hand over both horses. They did not appear to be hurt, and the wagon was in one piece. They did seem to be glad to see him. He was so relieved to find them that he wished he had a treat for them in his pocket. But a more urgent matter was on his mind. He got up on the wagon seat and took hold of the reins.

As he got the horses moving, he thought, *I hope the water goes down fast. Cora must be seen by the doctor just as soon as we can get her there.*

Everyone gave exclamations of joy when they heard the squeak of the wagon wheels. Carefully, Cora was helped into the wagon. Then the rest of the family got in, making sure they did not bump Cora's arm. If the water was not so deep, they could be on their way. They waited. At least, the storm was over and everything was peacefully quite now except for the occasional sounds made by the horses as they munched on the grass.

A few hours passed. Uncle John said that he was going to walk over to the creek and see if he could tell how much the water had gone down. He got off the wagon and disappeared into the darkness. He returned soon with water dripping off of him, but he felt sure they could ford the creek now. Aunt Jane checked Cora and made her as comfortable as possible. Everyone else knew to be still and hold onto the wagon while they crossed the stream. A couple of times, the wagon wheels shifted on some rocks in the creek, giving everyone a scare.

Once they were across the creek, Uncle John let the horses go at their own pace. They would sense danger if the wind had blown something in their way. Besides, the slower pace made it more bearable for Cora. On and on, they traveled through the night.

A considerable time later, Uncle John drove the wagon into the yard of the doctor's house. Even though it was in the middle of the night, someone was up. Lantern light shone through the windows. Uncle John jumped off the wagon and rushed up to the front door. Almost immediately, the doctor's wife opened the door. She listened as Uncle John explained why they were there.

The lady said, "Bring her in. The doctor will look see her. He has just returned from seeing a child on the farm next to ours, who was also injured in the storm. Just as soon as he washes his hands, he will be in here." As Uncle John turned toward the wagon, the doctor's wife called out to him, "Mr. Neighbors, bring the rest of your family inside. I'm sure they could use a cup of hot chocolate and something to eat. They can rest while the doctor examines Cora."

Uncle John gratefully accepted the lady's invitation for his family to go inside. He quickly returned to the wagon and helped his family. By the time they had gone into the house and washed up, the doctor's wife had their food ready to eat. After Uncle John had eaten, the doctor's wife told him that there was hay and grain in the barn if he wished to give some to his horses. Uncle John was a firm believer in taking good care of his animals. He expressed his appreciation once more and went outside to tend to his horses.

Several hours later, the doctor had repaired Cora's arm the best that he could. He told Aunt Jane and Uncle John to watch for signs of infection since some time had lapsed from the time the board entered her arm until it was removed. Cora looked very pale and was in quite a lot of pain. The doctor gave her something, and before long, she was able to eat a little food. The doctor suggested that since the other children were asleep on pallets the doctor's wife had prepared, that the family stay until daylight at least. He said that he really wanted to keep an eye on Cora's arm for several hours anyhow.

Aunt Jane and Uncle John felt that they would forever be indebted to the doctor and his wife for their kindness. The doctor's bill, Uncle John could pay, but the extra things they did to make him and his family feel comfortable would not be forgotten.

Some hours later, Uncle John gathered his family together, and thanking the doctor and his wife, the family got into the wagon. They headed for home, not knowing if their house would be standing or if the livestock had survived the tornado. The least of Aunt Jane's worries was her lovely flower bed.

The distance back to their house seemed twice as long as usual. All along the way, they saw damage from the tornado. It was shocking to see how the wind had twisted and torn so much. As they continued on their way, they became even more concerned about their house.

At last, they rounded the curve where their property line began. No one spoke a word. All eyes were focused toward the home place. Then there it was. What a beautiful sight it was too. The house was standing and apparently undamaged. Shouts of joy rang out as the wagon was brought to a stop not far from the front door. Everyone— except Cora, Aunt Jane, and Uncle John—eagerly got out of the wagon and ran into the house. Cora moved slowly, getting out of the wagon with her father helping her. Shortly, they had joined the rest of the family going through every room of the house to be sure everything was okay. While they were doing that, Uncle John went outside to see about the livestock and barn.

Later when the family gathered around the kitchen table to eat, they joined hands as the blessing was asked. Everyone was thankful they had come through the tornado and that Cora was not more seriously injured. They were grateful that they still had a house to come back to. It had been a frightening time, but they had a lot to be thankful for too.

That tornado was remembered for a long time by the people in that area. For years, signs of the tornado damage remained visible.

Cora recovered from her injury, but she had a stiff arm for the rest of her life.

This was just one of the many stories Aunt Jane shared with me, but it was the one I always asked to hear over and over.

What Is in That Big Box?

My childhood birthdays were always fun. Our house would be full of children dressed up in their Sunday best with instruction from their mothers to play careful and, above all, to avoid getting a tear or stain on their clothes. Mother and Mammaw always decorated the house with ribbons and balloons, but the dining room always got special treatment. Mammaw made the crocheted tablecloth, which was used only for special occasions and now dressed up the dining table. My mouth began to water as I saw the eatable decorations on the yummy-looking double-layer cake. Then I gazed over the cards and presents on the table. They were so beautifully wrapped and topped with large, bright bows.

My fifth birthday stands out in my mind. With the happy approval of my family, I invited a special guest, Miss Louise Durham, principal of Central School where later I was a student. The school was then located on Port Arthur Street across from Janssen Park. Not only did I attend all six grades there, but both my parents finished their first six grades there also. The school relocated, and in 1964, the First Baptist Church began construction on the old school grounds for a new church building and is still there today.

Miss Durham taught school for many years before becoming principal. As principal, she entered our classroom one day when I was in the third grade. Our teacher walked out of the room. The entire class wondered what was happening.

Miss Durham smiled and said, "I am going to babysit all of you for the next few minutes. Your teacher has stepped out into the hall to tell her boyfriend goodbye because he is leaving to go to war (This was WWII)."

In a few moments, our teacher came back into the classroom, and Miss Durham returned to her office. Thankfully, the boyfriend survived the war, returned home, and married our teacher.

Well, there sat Miss Durham right next to our dining table. I was having fun playing games with the other children. From time to time, I would look over at the dining table where a large box had been placed among the other presents. I had asked for only one thing for my birthday, and I kept wondering if that big box might contain what I had wished for. Mammaw was handing out prizes to the winners of the games when the doorbell rang. Mother worked her way through a room filled with active children and opened the door. Mr. Plaster, the local photographer, walked in carrying a large bag. He owned a picture studio on Main Street and, over the years, had taken studio pictures of nearly everybody in town. He was going to take a group picture and then take a picture of me standing by Miss Durham, where she was still seated by the dining table.

It would take Mr. Plaster a little time to get the camera and tripod set up, so Mother suggested that I open my presents. All the children stood around the table as I headed for that big box. Mother casually picked up one of the other presents and placed it in front of me. After opening the gift again, I reached for the big box. Mother stepped into my view and, while smiling, moved her head in a "no" movement. Finally I realized that she wanted me to open my guests' presents before opening family gifts. As I opened each present and thanked each person for what they had given me, I kept wondering what was in that big box. At last, all presents were open and sitting on the dining table. Eagerly, I reached for *that* big box. I thought I would never get the wrapping paper and bow off. I lifted the lid and folded the tissue paper back, and there was the most beautiful ice-skating doll I could ever imagine. She had golden-blond hair and a lovely white ice-skating outfit with red trim. Her ice skates were white, and the blades looked real, but they didn't cut my hands. I thought she was the most beautiful doll I had ever seen, especially since that was what I had wished for.

Mr. Plaster was ready to take the pictures. He had quite a time getting all the children placed just right so each one could be seen through the camera lens. Finally with everyone placed, he walked back to his camera, put a cloth over his head, and looked through the camera lens. Mother and Mammaw went to the kitchen to prepare refreshments of birthday cake and punch for the children. After a few minutes, Mother stepped back into the dining room to see how the picture taking was coming along.

Refreshments were ready, and Mother invited Mr. Plaster to join us. He replied that he had been eyeing that lovely cake since he saw it on the table, and he sure would appreciate a sample. Mr. Plaster told Mother that he had taken two pictures of the group and was ready to take the picture of Miss Durham and me. Suddenly Mother realized that I was not there. A quick search and Mother located me in Mammaw and Pappaw's bedroom playing with my new doll.

Mother said, "Do you know your guests are wondering where you are, and you missed the group picture. Come on now and get your picture with Miss Durham."

Mother and I went through the kitchen, and Mother told Mammaw where I was, then we reentered the dining room. Mother and Mammaw rearranged the children while Mr. Plaster took the picture of Miss Durham and me.

After that, Mr. Plaster had the task of getting the refreshment-filled children to be still long enough for him to take another picture. It had been quite a day—one I would not forget nor would Mother or Mammaw. And I dare say that Mr. Plaster would remember more than his piece of cake!

Bringing in the Flag

I was changing my clothes and combing my hair as fast as I could. Mother and I were going to town, and I hoped that we would be going to the post office.

Mama and Papa Borders worked as custodians at the post office. It was the most impressive structure on Mena's Main Street. Completed in 1917, it was made of buff brick and had four columns framing the front entrance. Around the perimeter of the roof were decorative posts, which stood seventeen inches high. Back some distance from the edge of the roof were four posts, identical to the ones around the edge of the roof. These four posts formed a square. Inside that square was a flagpole where the American flag was flown. That flag was the reason I hoped that Mother and I might be going to the post office.

The post office provided great adventure for me. Many times, Mother and I were there when it would be time for Papa Borders to go up on the roof and take down the American flag and bring it into the building for the night. He always asked if I would like to go with him. I looked at Mother for permission. Her answer was the same each time, yes. I turned back to Papa Borders with a big grin on my face and vigorously nodded my head up and down. Then my adventure began.

Directly below the window marked "STAMPS" were two wooden panels. They could only be opened from the other side. As they opened, I squatted down and scooted through the opening. Then the panels were closed behind me. The mail room was fascinating to me. There were men working everywhere. In some parts of the room were cabinets which contained small compartments called pigeon-holes. Some of the workers put mail into those small holes. Others took the mailbags out of very large canvas carts on wheels and sorted the sacks of mail. It was a busy place.

Papa Borders took my hand and led me through that room into another smaller room, which also contained bags of mail. We walked across that room, and he opened a door to the stairway. It was very dark on the stairs, but he always held onto me. He reached up and took hold of a long cord. Suddenly the whole stairway was lit up. We went on up the stairs until we came to another door. Papa Borders opened that door, and we stepped out onto the roof of the post office. I was always told to stand right by the door until Papa Borders lowered the flag and folded it. Then he would tuck the flag under his arm and walk over to me. Taking my hand, we walked over fairly close to the edge of the roof. It was so exciting to look down on the sidewalk and Main Street. From our vantage point, I could even see over the rooftops of some of the buildings. I felt like I was on top of the world. I was glad those decorative posts were there along the edge of the roof, however. After a few minutes, we left the roof and returned to the workroom downstairs. I thanked Papa Borders for taking me with him and told him goodbye. The two wooden panels would be opened for me again, and I squatted down and scooted through the opening to the main lobby, where Mother was waiting for me. I never tired of going up on the roof of the post office with Papa Borders, and I enjoyed being with Papa and Mama Borders at their home.

They lived six blocks from our house and one block from the First Baptist Church, where we all attended. Going home with Papa and Mama Borders for Sunday dinner was special. Arriving at their house, the first thing Mama Borders did was to remove the long hat pin from her black Sunday hat. Then she carefully lifted the hat off her head. Pushing the hat pin through the brim of the hat, she opened the closet door of their bedroom and placed her hat on a shelf, where it would remain until the next Sunday. Next she put an apron on over her one Sunday dress. She would busy herself in the kitchen for a few minutes before saying, "Dinner is ready, let's eat."

Mama Borders always used a beautiful lacy tablecloth, her fine dishes, and silver. Then with all the food on the table, we could hardly wait for the blessing to be asked. Mama Borders was a good cook. I enjoyed everything she fixed, but over the years, my favorites were her mashed potatoes, cornbread, and her two-layered white cake. She used coarse ground pepper in her potatoes, and I do not know what else she put in them, but they were fluffy and very tasty.

She used her cast-iron skillet to bake the cornbread. When it was done, she removed it from the oven and tipped the skillet sideways. The golden-brown cornbread slid out of the skillet onto a plate. It was served piping hot with butter. It was so good; I could have made a meal of it.

Mama Borders was known for her white cake. She always made a layer cake with a pineapple filling that she spread between the layers. Then she covered the cake with a creamy, rich, white icing, topped with moist coconut. It was so good; it melted in my mouth.

Mama Borders' hair had turned silvery white by the time she was twenty-one years old. I always thought it was beautiful. She wore it in a large round bun on the back of her head, secured by long hairpins.

Mama Borders had an old black pot in their backyard, where she made lye soap. She always put something in it to make it smell good. The lye soap was multipurpose. She used it for their laundry, and she used it for her shampoo. One time, a friend had gone to the doctor with a rash that would not go away.

The doctor said, "Well, what would do you the most good is some old-fashioned lye soap, but I don't know where you could get any."

That person got some of Mama Borders' lye soap, and the rash disappeared, never to reoccur.

Mama Borders always had a basket on the floor by her rocking chair. It was full of crochet and embroidery work. She never sat down that she was not working on something. She made many pairs of lovely pillowcases, tea towels, afghans, and aprons. All of them showed her neat and attractive handiwork.

On one occasion, Mama and Papa Borders had their picture taken at Mr. Plaster's Studio. Mama Borders wore her Sunday dress, adorned with a lovely cameo pin. Papa Borders was in his Sunday suit. The picture was a very good likeness of them.

Papa Borders kept their yard very trim and neat. I liked to watch him use the edger along the sidewalk. The flower beds never showed a weed or wilted bloom. Spearmint grew near their back door, and when it was sprayed with water from the garden hose, a pleasant aroma wafted through the air.

Some years ago, a new post office was built in Mena, and the old one was converted into City Hall. A flagpole was placed on the ground in front of the building. While the decorative posts remain around the perimeter of the roof of the structure, those four posts forming the square for the flagpole were removed. I have one of those posts in my home, which serves as a constant reminder of my adventure of going on the roof with Papa Borders.

Many years have passed now, and Mama and Papa Borders are no longer living. A number of years before she died, Mama Borders gave me the cameo broach that she wore in the picture. I treasure it, wearing it often. I still have aprons, pillowcases, and tea towels made by Mama Borders. I use the pillowcases on special occasions and always receive compliments on them. Mama and Papa Borders were a special part of my childhood.

The Orange Dot

During the forties, when I was a child, a different margarine was developed. It came in a plastic bag not quite the size of a sheet of notebook paper. In the middle of that bag was a small orange dot. You had to press that dot and massage the bag to get the orange color blended in. My dad suggested that he and I go to the living room, which was rather long, and play toss until the margarine was well mixed.

We did this each time Mother got a new bag. On one occasion, we were playing toss, and I had the bag in hand ready to make a Major League throw. I reared back and sent that bag sailing through the air. *Whack!* Daddy missed my toss, and it landed near the top of the old upright piano, bursting the plastic bag, and unblended margarine drizzled down the front of the piano. Now this piano had a rough surface, and the goo found every tiny crevice. Mother appeared at the living room when she heard the whack sound. The expression on her face put the idea in my head that now was a great time to go play in the backyard, but her eyes told me I had better stay put. Daddy looked rather sheepish. Mother walked over to the piano, examined the mess, and immediately gave us detailed instruction on how to clean the piano. Then she added in a parental tone that we find a spot *outside* to get that orange dot blended in.

Daddy pulled the piano cover over the keys, got the bucket, cleaning solution, two rags, and we began rubbing and cleaning. It took a long time to clean out all those tiny crevices, but finally, the piano looked good as new, and we never did play toss with a margarine bag in the house again.

The Fishing Trip

I enjoyed an enriched and delightful childhood. Pappaw and Daddy co-owned a grocery store, and it was a fascinating place to me. There were very few unhappy moments in my childhood, but during the early summer of 1943, when I was six years old, I had a most unusual experience.

During the WWII years, the Mena businessmen closed their doors at noon every Wednesday to give people time to work in their Victory Gardens. On one of those Wednesdays, our family decided to spend the afternoon fishing and enjoying a picnic supper on the riverbank. I even had my own cane pole, cut down to my size.

Mammaw and Mother were in the kitchen preparing fried chicken, potato salad, chocolate cake, and other picnic goodies when Daddy told Mother through the kitchen window that he was going down to Hub's Produce and get some chicken entrails for fish bait.

Hub and Helen Frye, longtime family friends, owned and operated a chicken produce business where they killed and cleaned chickens. All of the entrails and smelly, slick, sticky goo was piped into a large, round vat outside the building. A board was kept across the top of the vat.

When I heard Daddy say he was going someplace, not having anything to do, I asked if I could go. He nodded yes and told Mother that I was going with him. In a few minutes, we were turning into Hub's place of business. Daddy told me to remain in the truck as he would be right back. To a six-year-old, the term "right back" can be used up quickly. As I sat there in the truck, the bright summer sun was shining through the windshield in full force. I was wearing a brand-new pair of white summer sandals with shiny brass buckles. As only a six-year-old might do, I became concerned that the heat would make my feet sweat, causing the buckles to rust. After what seemed like a long time, I did something very unusual for me—I disobeyed Daddy.

After I got out of the truck, I stood there and looked for a way to get into the building. I saw no door on that side, but there were a lot of crates and other things lying all around. I decided I was going to have to cross that vat to enter the building. I made my way over to the vat, carefully stepped upon a crate, and got up on the board that spanned the top of the vat. I do not know how deep that vat was, but when I fell in it, the smelly, slick, stinky goo came up to my chin.

I immediately called out for Daddy. In seconds, he came running out of the building with Hub and Helen right behind him. The three of them managed to pull me out of that terrible muck onto dry ground. Hub and Helen were having a great deal of difficulty keeping a straight face. Daddy's expression, on the other hand, would have made "The Great Stone Face" look like a laughing face. In fact, I was sure that I saw Daddy's eyes sparking fire. When he uttered not a single word to me but just pointed to the truck, I began to suspect that I was in serious trouble.

I tried to walk to the truck, but my sandals were as slimy as I was. Daddy walked over and lowered the tailgate of the truck then waited for me to get in the truck bed. That was no easy task. My hands were so slick that I just kept sliding off. After several futile attempts, I turned around and looked at Daddy. Hub and Helen were still fighting a losing battle to keep from laughing out loud. It took only one quick glance at Daddy for me to know that I would be getting no help from him. Somehow I would have to get my smelly self up in the truck bed by myself.

I guess I had rubbed and pulled enough to get some of that goo off my hands. At long last, I was successful in getting up into the truck bed. Daddy shut the tailgate with what I thought was an overly firm slam. It was my thought to get down low in the truck bed so no one could see me in such a mess. Actually, I had no choice. There was no possible way I could have sat up with that slimy goo all over me. All the way home, I just knew that every vehicle we met got a strong whiff of the terrible odor coming from the truck bed. It was a long, miserable ride.

I did not dare try to rise up enough to look over the side of the truck bed, but I felt the truck slow down and then Daddy turned into our driveway. As I heard him turn off the engine and get out of the truck, I wondered what my fate was going to be.

Daddy walked to the back of the truck and, again, lowered the tailgate. I slid out faster than usual but managed to land on my feet. As I started for the front door, Daddy stepped in front of me, but not too close, and without a word, pointed to the backyard. By now, I was definitely feeling like an abandoned orphan. Daddy, always quick to laugh, had a facial expression that could stop a freight train. I walked down our driveway to the backyard. I heard Daddy coming at a safe distance behind me. In the backyard, Daddy picked up the garden hose, adjusted the nozzle to a narrow but forceful stream, and pointed it straight at me. I realized then that my troubles had just begun. He began spraying the water at my chin and worked his way down. It felt like a hundred pins pricking my skin. It seemed that the slick stuff just slid around on me. Finally Daddy turned off the water and walked to the back door of our house, where he called out for Mother to come outside. She appeared at the door wiping her hands on a hand towel. When she saw me standing there with water pouring off of me, her facial expression changed considerably, and she asked what in the world had happened. Before I could open my mouth, Daddy began telling Mother the whole story of how I came to be in such a condition. I thought the vat ordeal was pretty bad, but he made it sound even worse.

When he finally finished, Mother said, "Well, what she needs now is a good bath."

I thought, *Thank goodness, a fun time playing in the tub.* Besides, I was looking forward to some quiet time all by myself.

Mother peeled off my slimy, soaking-wet clothes, removed my pitiful-looking sandals, and left it all on the back steps. She marched me to the bathroom where she filled the tub with water that was plenty warm. To this, she added a very generous portion of bubble bath. When I sat down in the tub, the suds came up to the exact spot that the chicken goo had come to. My dream of a quiet time alone was replaced by Mother getting on her knees right next to the tub. She rubbed and scrubbed. Then she leaned close to me and took a sniff. Then she scrubbed some more. She scrubbed for so long that my skin was pink and tingling. After a thorough rinsing, she gave me a brisk rub down with a towel, wrapped the towel around me, and tucked in the corner. She immediately plopped my head down in the lavatory and began shampooing my hair. Now Mother had shampooed my hair and rolled it every Saturday for as long as I could remember. We always did it on Saturday, so it would be clean and nice looking for Sunday School and Church on Sunday. Never, not one time in all my recollection, could I remember Mother rubbing so hard. Now my head felt just like the rest of me, tingling.

Finally Mother handed me a towel to get the excess water out of my hair.

As I was very gently rubbing my hair, Mother said, "Now, young lady, I am going to go and lay out some clean clothes for you to put on. See if you can stay out of trouble while we finish getting things ready to go."

I had never had such words spoken to me before, and I felt like my world had fallen completely apart.

As Mother returned to the kitchen to help Mammaw, I hurried to my bedroom and got dressed as quickly as I could because I had another problem to deal with, my sandals. I rushed through the house and out the back door. There on the back step were two very pitiful-looking sandals that used to be white. I did not have to bend over to know that they did not smell good. I noticed that my wet clothes, so recently removed from me, were nowhere to be seen. In fact, I never saw those clothes again. I moved over a little distance and sat down on another step to think of how I could fix my sandals.

The idea came to me that what had been effective on me might work for my shoes. Very carefully picking them up by the least touch, I headed for the bathroom. Filling the lavatory with water as hot as my hands could take, I added a lot of bubble bath and getting a stiff brush I got to work on those sandals. I did just as Mother had done—I scrubbed, rubbed, and sniffed. Then I did it all over again.

With my arms aching, I rinsed the sandals, towel dried them, and examined my efforts. It was not enough. The chicken smell was still very much there. Walking through the house, I thought and thought about something I could do to get rid of that awful smell. As I walked through Mother and Daddy's bedroom, I saw a full bottle of cologne on top of their chest of drawers. It seemed to me that a bit of cologne just might take care of my smelly sandal problem. I got the bottle, removed the lid, and put a dab of cologne on the inside of the heel strap. One tiny dab did nothing, so I kept dabbing more and more. Before I knew it, the bottle was empty. Now the whole room reeked of cologne.

I figured that the best thing for those sandals was sunshine and fresh air, a lot of fresh air. I picked them up and made my way to the back steps. The fragrance of cologne must have wafted through the house because as I went outside, I heard Daddy say, "Opal, come see what Lee (my nickname) has done now." I increased my speed out into the backyard but heard parts of their conversation as they got nearer. Words such as "All gone, not a drop of Chanel Number Five left."

Whatever Chanel Number Five was, I knew that I was in deeper trouble. A short time ago, I had not thought that was possible.

Just at that moment, Pappaw came around the corner of the house and said, "I am going down to the store and check on some things before we leave for the river. Lee is going with me."

I was already halfway to the car. Moments later, we arrived at the store. As we got out of the car, I looked up and down Main Street. It seemed so strange to not see people or cars anywhere. Pappaw unlocked the door, and we went in. He turned on the lights and the ceiling fans. He walked around and looked here and there. After a few moments, he said that he was ready to go. Then we drove around town. Pappaw commented on that new house going up or an addition to someone's house. After a while, he headed for home. When we arrived, everything was ready to load for our fishing trip and picnic supper.

As we started getting into the car, Pappaw said, "Lee is going to sit by me because I am going to give her some fishing pointers." He talked all the way to the fishing hole.

I could hear the musical ripple of the water as we drove up near the river.

As we unloaded everything, Pappaw remarked, "Now Lee and I are going over there by that big tree to do our fishing."

Mammaw found a good spot just a short way from us, and Mother and Daddy settled in just beyond Mammaw's place.

Pappaw and I sat there for what seemed to me a very long time. Finally I began talking. Immediately, Pappaw quietly told me that everyone must be quiet, or the sound of our voices would scare the fish away. I started counting clouds, ants, rocks, and the bugs that landed on top of the water.

Suddenly Pappaw exclaimed, "Lee, Lee! You have a fish. Don't let him get away."

I replied, "You get it for me."

He grabbed the pole and set the hook. By the way Pappaw was working with that fish, I expected him to bring in a ten-pound bass. However, I thought the tiny rainbow perch was just beautiful. I asked Pappaw if it was big enough to keep because Mammaw had a rule about keeping small fish. He assured me that it was indeed big enough to keep. How Mammaw scraped, cleaned, and cooked that small fish I will never know, but it tasted good to me.

When everyone had their fill of fishing, we enjoyed a tasty supper there by the river. Before I knew it, the sun was setting, and it was time to go home. The drive back to the house was uneventful, but I kept wondering if I was still in trouble.

Later that evening, after I went to bed, I laid there and thought over the most unusual day I had ever had. I never got a spanking for my disobeying Daddy's instructions or using all of Mother's expensive perfume. In fact, the events were not mentioned then or later. However, I did not need a spanking as I was punished enough by having to wear those awful sandals all that summer.

One recollection of the day continues to bring a smile to my face.

As I laid in bed, I thought to myself, *Pappaw, I will keep it a secret, but that fish was on your fishing pole, not mine.* I kept that secret until the day Pappaw died.

Footnote: I made mention that this story took place during the WWII years. A few days after the above story occurred, Mother, Daddy, and I boarded a train in Mena, which took us to Kansas City, Missouri. We stayed overnight in a hotel. The next day, Daddy boarded another train for New York, where he entered the military service. That same day, Mother and I returned to Mena by train.

A Special Trip to New Orleans

In July of 1945, Daddy called Mother from New Orleans. He asked if she and I could come for a short time. Mother replied that we could. On July 23, we boarded the Kansas City Southern Railroad bound for New Orleans. I do not remember much about the trip, except that we got to eat in the dining car, and I found that quite fun. When we arrived, Aunt Thelma met us at the station as Uncle Spence was stationed in New Orleans at that time. She drove us to the Colonial Courts, where Daddy had reserved rooms for us because Aunt Thelma and Uncle Spence were also staying there. It was nice to have them just a few doors away from us.

The Colonial Court was shaped like a horseshoe with a play-ground in the center. There was a loudspeaker that sounded forth music and frequent news bulletins. The highway was near, and I enjoyed seeing horse-drawn wagons hauling the biggest bananas I had ever seen.

That evening, Daddy came and told us this story. His merchant marine ship was in port for repairs. It was not known how long this would take. He explained to us that when he left each morning to report to his ship, that if the repair work was completed, the ship with full crew would depart and return to the Pacific. He would not be allowed to call and tell us goodbye because of national security reasons. So every morning, Mother and I would say goodbye and wonder all day if we would see him that evening.

Sometimes after supper, Uncle Spence, Aunt Thelma, Mother, Daddy, and I would do a little sightseeing around the city. It sure was a big place, and we did a lot of walking. One evening, we were strolling along, and I was just a few steps ahead. I had a habit of walking on my tiptoes. Most of the time, I was not conscious of doing this; it just came naturally.

I heard Aunt Thelma, who was always very outspoken, say, "If she was my girl, I would break her of walking that way."

I wondered what Daddy would say. He replied, "Well, it has not harmed Linda in any way, and it does not bother me. So I guess I will let her keep on walking that way."

Aunt Thelma did not say anything else, so I figured that Uncle Spence must have made a rather bold move and had given her a nudge to hush.

The days passed and I spent a lot of time each day in the play area. Several other children were there, and we all had fun playing together. Every evening for three weeks, just about supper time, Daddy came back to the motel. Then everything changed.

I was in the play area having a good time with the other children. The loudspeaker was playing music as usual. Then suddenly, the music stopped. There was total silence. We children became still and waited to see what would happen.

The radio announcer said, "Ladies and gentlemen, in a moment, you will hear an announcement from the president of the United States."

Again, there was a pause. I stood there and waited.

In a moment, the radio announcer said, "Ladies and gentlemen, I give you the president of the United States, Harry S. Truman."

He stated that the war was over. "Japan had surrendered, and there would be a formal signing of surrender aboard the *USS battleship Missouri* on September 2, 1945 in Tokyo Bay."

I ran to our motel room, yelling to Mother that the war was over.

Mother said, "Oh, you must be mistaken."

I assured her that I had heard correctly.

She said, "Let's go to Aunt Thelma's room and see if she has heard anything."

We rushed to her door and knocked. She did not have her radio on but quickly turned it on, but by that time, we could hear bells ringing, horns honking, and whistles blowing. People were coming out of their motel rooms jumping up and down, shouting at the top of their lungs. Everyone was laughing and crying at the same time. It was a time no one would ever forget.

That evening, Daddy came back to the motel. Then we relived the good news all over again. He said that Mother and I would have to return to Mena without him because he had to wait to be formally discharged. He expected to be home within a week.

That night, Mother packed our things, and the next morning, we told Daddy goodbye, but oh my! How happy that goodbye was compared to the past three weeks. Later that day, Aunt Thelma drove us to the train station where we boarded the KCS for home. Sure enough, within a week, Daddy arrived back home fully discharged. Life could gradually return to normal now.

Postscript: During Daddy's training in New York prior to going overseas, he met another merchant marine named Louie Belanti, a very big Italian. His folks lived near the base, and they invited Daddy over for an authentic Italian supper. As he and Louie left to report back to their base, Daddy thanked Louie's folks for a good meal. After the war, Daddy and Louie kept in touch. One day, when I came home from school, Mother said that Daddy had invited Louie to come for a visit. I looked forward to meeting this man who had been with Daddy throughout the war.

The day he arrived was exciting. He was friendly and seemed at ease with all of us. One evening while Louie was with us, Mother prepared Italian spaghetti.

I was very impressed at the amount of spaghetti and meat sauce that Louie put on his plate and said, "Mother, you are going to have to get him another plate."

While Mother was discretely shushing me, Daddy said something to cover my remark. After a few days, Louie said goodbye to everyone, told us what a good time he had and how pretty it was here. He gave us a hearty invitation to come and visit him in New York. Daddy talked about it a few times, but we never made it up there. Some years later, Louie died.

Daddy was stationed at Sheepshead Bay, New York—along the Brooklyn coast.

My Softball Bat

Mother was calling to me through the open window of the living room to come in the house. It was such a nice day to be outside; I really did not want to leave the yard where I was playing. However, I suspected that Mother wanted me to do some more on that speech that I had to memorize. I slowly gathered up my playthings and went in.

Mother had the speech in her hand. She reminded me that in a couple of weeks, the Arkansas Baptist Training Union Convention would be held in Little Rock. I had been chosen by our church, the First Baptist Church in Mena, to give a speech. Mother had written the speech for me. It was about Paul.

She smiled at me and said, "We need to spend some more time on the last page. Now I am going to listen as you talk. Remember, do not talk too fast, and speak in a loud voice. The Baptist Church in Little Rock where you will be giving your speech has a large auditorium. You will want everyone to be able to hear you. Look at me as you speak. Don't look off somewhere. You will need to look at the people you will be speaking to."

We worked for a while on places I was not quite sure of. Finally Mother said that I could go play some more before supper would be ready.

Every day, Mother had me practice on the speech.

At last, the day came when she said, "You know it perfectly. There are several days yet before we will leave for Little Rock. We will go over it a few times each day, so you won't forget it."

I did know that speech. I knew it backward, forward, and from the middle to the end. Mother could start the speech anywhere, and

I could pick it up and finish it. At least now that I had it prepared, I could have more playtime.

A few days later, Mother, Mammaw, and I left Mena for Little Rock. Daddy and Pappaw stayed at our house. The trip to the capital city was exciting, and when we arrived in Little Rock, we checked into a hotel downtown. Then we went shopping. Mother and Mammaw bought new things for me from the skin out. I got a gray suit with a pretty white blouse. My new shoes were black patent Roman sandals. I felt very dressed up.

We ate an early supper in the hotel dining room that evening, so I would have time to change into my new outfit before we would to leave for the church. Mother wanted to have plenty of time to drive us there.

As we drove into the parking area, I thought, *Boy! this is a big church.*

I was glad Mother had insisted on having me speak so loudly when I practiced the speech at home. We went inside and found seats. The pulpit area was on a raised platform which curved in a half-circle design. There was a low railing around the edge of the platform. Soon the program began. It seemed only minutes before I heard my name being announced. I left my seat, walked up on the platform, and began my speech.

I remembered the things Mother had cautioned me about. I saw an elderly gentleman seated in the back of the auditorium. I looked at him frequently. I decided if he looked like he was hearing me okay, then probably everyone else was hearing me too. I glanced at Mother and Mammaw every once in a while as they were sitting close to the front of the church. At one time, Mother frowned slightly but quickly smiled at me.

Mammaw smiled throughout my speech. I finished with relief and knew that I had not forgotten any of it. It was very unlikely that I would forget with as much practice as Mother had made me do on it. I returned to my seat, and the program continued. At the conclusion, Mother and Mammaw came to me and commented on how well I delivered the speech. Then some people came by where I was standing and complimented me.

Later as Mother, Mammaw, and I were on our way back to the hotel, I asked Mother, "Why did you frown at me during the speech?"

Mother replied, "Honey, you did a very good job of presenting the speech, and we are proud of you. Were you aware that you rested one knee on the railing throughout the speech?"

I replied, "No, I did not realize I had done that. I was trying to remember to speak loud, to not speak too fast, and to look at the people. I guess I just was not thinking about my knees."

When we arrived at the hotel, we went to our room. It had been a long day, and we were ready for a good night's sleep. I did not go to sleep immediately, however. I laid there and listened to the noises of the city—sirens blaring, horns honking, and traffic moving about on the street.

After a few minutes, I relaxed and thought, *I'm glad that speech is over.*

The next thing I knew, it was morning.

We got dressed and went down to the dining room for breakfast. I found it interesting to watch the waiters and waitresses move about to serve everyone. One waitress came by our table carrying a very large, round tray loaded with dishes of food. I feared that she would spill everything that was on that tray before she got to the people waiting for the food. To my relief, she served every dish that was on that tray without a single spill. When our meal arrived, it was tasty, and we enjoyed it. I continued to watch with interest as other people entered and left the dining room.

After eating, we returned to our room and got our things together for the trip back to Mena.

A short time later as we were getting into our car, Mother said, "Linda, we are going shopping before we start for home."

I replied, "We went shopping just yesterday."

Mother smiled and responded, "I know, but this shopping trip is a fun one. You were so good to come in the house to work on your speech, and you never complained. I knew you wanted to be outside playing, but the hard work paid off. You did a very good job. Now what would you like to have?"

I did not hesitate for one moment before stating, "A softball bat."

Mother and Mammaw looked at each other, somewhat surprised. I was sure that they thought I would ask for something other than a bat. After searching for a little while, we found a sporting goods store, parked the car, and went in. A man came up to us and asked if he could be of any help. Mother told him we were interested in a softball bat.

He looked at me and asked, "Is it for this young lady?"

Mother told him that it was. I looked around the store. I had never seen so many bats in my life. There were rows and rows of them. The man walked over to one of the rows and removed the first bat. He looked at it and then looked at me. He held it in both of his hands and appeared to be considering the weight of it.

Finally he handed the bat to me and said, "Try this one and see how it feels to you."

I looked at the bat. It was smaller than the other bats on that one rack. It was maroon in color, and I thought it was the best-looking bat in the world.

I took it in my hands and thought, *I like the way this bat feels.*

Even though I was of a small frame, I was sure that I could handle that bat. I lifted it then looked around me.

The man smiled and said, "Go ahead, swing it. You have plenty of room."

I swung the bat as though a ball was coming right at me. I was amazed at how quickly that bat sliced through the air. I looked up at Mother.

She just smiled and said to the man, "We'll take it."

Mother paid for the bat, then going out to the car, she asked me if I would like to put it in the trunk. I told her that I would just keep it with me. I could hardly wait until we arrived back home. I was anxious to show Daddy and Pappaw my bat.

The trip back home was relaxing. I did not have to keep the speech in my mind now. I enjoyed looking out of the car window as we drove along, but most of all, I was happy because I had my own bat.

A few hours later, Mother turned the car into our driveway and stopped. I saw Daddy and Pappaw come out on the front porch. In seconds, I was out of the car with the bat in my hand.

I ran up to them and said, "Look, I have a bat."

Daddy remarked about what a good-looking bat it was and replied, "Let's go in the backyard and put it to use."

I do not know how long we stayed in the backyard while Daddy pitched me one ball after the other. That bat sure felt good in my hands.

After a while, Daddy and I sat down to rest.

He asked, "What made you want a bat?"

I replied, "At school during recess, we play softball. I am the smallest person in my class, and no matter how hard I try, I can never get the ball past the pitcher's mound. Daddy, I am a sure out every time I step up to the batter's box. Both teams have agreed that someone else can bat for me, and I can run the bases. Now I could do my own hitting."

The thought made me feel ten feet tall.

Daddy smiled when I explained about recess and said, "I bet you knock the ball far enough to get you to first base now." Then he asked me about the trip to Little Rock.

I told him that I remembered all of the speech. I did not talk too fast, and I kept my voice loud so everyone could hear me. I even looked at the people as I spoke. Then I told him how I had propped one of my knees on the railing the entire time I was talking. He just chuckled about that and said he was very proud of me. I told him that in addition to the bat, I got all new clothes to wear for that special event. He said that he would like to see them, so I got the suit, blouse, and shoes. He remarked about how nice they looked and that they would make a very nice-looking Sunday School outfit. Then he said we had better go in the house as it was getting late. I picked up my new things, and we went in to join the rest of the family. It had been an exciting day, and I was tired.

I took my bat to school with me every day. What a thrill it was to smack that ball and see it go sailing past first base. No one had to hit the ball for me now. When school let out in the afternoons, I took my bat home with me. In fact, that bat was such a treasure, I slept with it, hard as it was, for quite a long time. It continued to be a treasure long after I graduated from elementary school.

The Winter of 1948

It was December of 1948. I was in the fourth grade and feeling pretty proud of myself. I had never gone this far into a school year without missing several days due to illness. Just maybe, this would be the year I would reach my goal—to receive a certificate of perfect attendance at the end of the school year. That dream would last only two weeks longer.

What started out as influenza and a heart murmur quickly developed into double pneumonia and rheumatic fever. Our family physician, Dr. Stewart, had come to our house several times to see me. He now told my family—which consisted of my parents, maternal grandparents, whom I called Mammaw and Pappaw, and myself—that I needed to be in the hospital. He would go and make the necessary arrangements.

A short time later, we arrived at the hospital. Before we even got to my room, a nurse stopped us and offered me a glass of milk. I wanted none of that. I knew what it would do—the same thing everything else had done for the past several days, come back up.

I simply said, "No, thank you. I don't care for any."

She explained that I really needed to drink it. I told her that nothing stayed down, and my stomach was sore from everything coming back up.

She smiled and said, "I know you have had a bad time of it, but I promise you that this milk will stay down. Besides, the doctor wants you to drink it."

I reluctantly accepted the glass and took a very tiny sip. I was amazed. It stayed down. My stomach felt just a little bit better. I took another sip and then another. This was great. I looked down into the glass of milk; I sniffed it. It looked and tasted like milk, but what made it stay down?

While the nurse stood there, I drank it all, and as I handed her the empty glass, I asked, "What was in that milk?"

She smiled again and replied, "Oh, it is just plain milk."

I never did find out what made that milk special, but from then on, during my stay in the hospital, I accepted every glass of milk offered to me and drank it without question.

A few days after I entered the hospital, I developed yellow jaundice and scarlatina. Nurses were coming into my room more often now with stethoscope, thermometer, and additional medicine in hand.

Mother and Mammaw took turns staying with me during the day. Since Daddy and Pappaw co-owned a grocery store, they stopped by several times a day. They all took turns staying with me at night.

One day, Daddy brought a small carton of ice cream to my room. The nurse provided us with bowls and spoons. I asked the nurse if she could take a bowl of ice cream to the boy in the next room. He was a friend of mine and was recovering from pneumonia. The nurse gladly took the ice cream to him. Later she told me how much he had enjoyed it.

After I had eaten all I could hold, Daddy raised one of the windows in my room and placed the carton outside on the window ledge. It was cold enough outside that the ice cream stayed good until it was eaten up later that day. It was a fun treat.

I spent Christmas in the hospital that year. Daddy cut the top out of the Christmas tree at home. The family came to my room loaded down with the small decorated tree and presents. I opened a few of mine before becoming too tired. Daddy, Mammaw, and Pappaw took turns opening the rest of my packages while Mother arranged them on a table for me to look at.

Gradually, I began to improve. By this time, the nurses and I had become good friends, and they stopped by my room sometimes just to visit for a moment.

Finally I was able to go home. Dr. Stewart explained that I would have to go straight to bed, and he had arranged for a nurse to stay at our house for two weeks. She was to keep a record of my progress and give me a penicillin shot every two hours around the clock. I was given vitamins, calcium, iron, and liver shots. I already had quite an assortment of empty medicine bottles I kept under my bed in a long box which Daddy had brought from the store.

I was beginning to wonder when I would be allowed out of bed. So far, every time I asked the doctor about it, he just said, "It is too soon to talk about that." The tone of his voice made me think that I was not going to be getting out of bed any time soon. I thought of all the things I would do—ride my bike, climb my favorite tree in our side yard, and skate on the sidewalk. Boy, I was going to make up for lost time when I was allowed to get up.

Family and friends did many nice things to help me pass the time in bed. Dr. Stewart said that he did not want me trying to do any makeup work for school until he said it was okay. I thought he was the best doctor in the whole world. I had books, puzzles, View-Master with reels, board games, cards, and best of all, my family who took turns sitting by my bed telling me story after story.

For some time, I was not allowed to have any visitors. People telephoned to see how I was doing. I received cards through the mail, which I had propped up, so I could see them.

At last, when Dr. Stewart said it was okay for friends to come and see me; I was delighted. It was like a breath of fresh air to have a link with other people.

After several weeks, when Dr. Stewart came by the house one day and checked me over, he sat back in the chair that was always provided for him and smiled. I held my breath.

He looked at me and said, "Linda, if you continue like this for the next two weeks, you can get out of bed." He told me some other things, but the only thing I heard was "two weeks."

I would have liked it better if he had said I could get up right then, or tomorrow, but at least now, I had a goal to work toward.

Everyone put forth special effort to help me pass the time. Mother put little surprises on my meal trays. I always looked forward to them. Sometimes she would hide the surprise under my napkin then pretend she had forgotten it. We would have a laugh when I found the treat.

Sometimes it seemed that the two weeks would never pass. I would have even welcomed some schoolwork by this time. But then that very special day arrived. I was so excited. I could hardly wait until five o'clock when Dr. Stewart closed his office and began his house calls. I figured that he could be at our house by ten minutes after five. Surely he would come to see me first. From my bed, I had a good view of the street through the two windows in my room. I watched every car that drove past our house. I watched and waited. Supper time came and Mother brought my tray. She had worked especially hard to make it attractive for me, but it was difficult to think about eating anything. I just wanted out of that bed. It became dark outside. Daddy turned on the porch light, and I watched to see if any car headlights angled toward the curb. The family gathered around my bed and tried to entertain me. My mind just was not on the games. I kept my ears alert for the sound of a car that might be slowing down in front of our house. By nine o'clock, I had decided that he was not going to make it that night. Then I saw headlights go slower than normal.

I heard a car door shut, and I exclaimed, "He's here."

A moment later, Dr. Stewart walked into my bedroom, looking very tired. As everyone gathered around, he gave me such a thorough examination that I thought he would never get finished. Finally he leaned back in the chair by my bed, looked at me, and smiled. I thought his face looked encouraging, but I tried not to get my hopes up.

He said, "Linda, I know you have waited a long time for this, and you are a good patient. You can get out of bed."

I was on the floor in a second and took a step when I felt a firm grip on my arm. Startled, I turned my head toward the doctor.

He had a puzzled look on his face and asked, "Where are you going?"

I did not understand what was happening here. I replied, "You told me I could get up."

His expression changed from puzzled to pained. He picked me up and put me on his lap.

"Linda, I am so sorry that I did not make myself clear to you, but I did explain to you a couple of weeks ago that when I did let you out of bed, it would be for one step only. You have taken that step. You must get back in bed, so I can see how your heart reacted."

I slowly got back to bed. I barely heard Dr. Stewart say that he was pleased to observe that my heart was beating normal. He and my family went into the kitchen, where they sat around the table and talked of my progress. I turned over on my stomach, put my pillow over my head, and cried and cried. One step! I wondered if I would ever be free of that bed.

The next evening when Dr. Stewart came by, he checked me over and said that I could take two steps. Then it was back in bed for another heart check. It was beating normal. Each day when the doctor came, he examined me then added another step to what I had taken the day before. Over a period of time, I built up enough strength to go throughout the house. I felt like a bird out of a cage.

I continued to make progress. It was slow but steady. Then came a really special day. Dr. Stewart told me he had made his last visit to our house.

"Young lady, you are coming to my office tomorrow instead of me coming here."

I nearly shouted.

He continued, "I have waited to have you come to my office since it is upstairs over the drugstore. I wanted to be sure that you were ready to climb those stairs. Now when you arrive at my office, you are to tell my receptionist immediately because I want to check your heart."

I told him I would remember.

The next day, Mother and I made the trip to Dr. Stewarts's office. We went upstairs, and immediately, the receptionist took me back to one of the examining rooms. Dr. Stewart was there and checked my heart. I could tell by the look on his face that the report was going to be good, and it was.

Gradually the trips to the doctor's office were stretched farther and farther apart until I was only going once a week. He still kept a close check on me. Over the next year, I continued to get stronger. I was allowed to slowly ease back into the activities I had been involved in before I got sick. Dr. Stewart and my family maintained a constant watch over me, however.

In spite of their good care, there were times that I became ill. It seemed I always developed a fever during the night.

Daddy would pick up the telephone, and when the operator asked, "Number please," Daddy would give her Dr. Stewart's home telephone number.

She would always ask, "Charles, is Linda sick again?"

Daddy would say that I was.

"Well," the operator said, "it won't do any good for me to call his home because he has been called out. Right now, he is at Mr. Key's house. His heart is acting up pretty bad tonight. I'll just call their house and have them tell the doctor to come to your house next."

He always came, no matter the hour. We knew he was on his way because he had someone at the house he was leaving to call our house. This let Mother or Mammaw know to put a pan of water on the stove to boil. When Dr. Stewart arrived, he would sterilize his syringe as he had to use it over and over again.

I experienced no heart damage from the rheumatic fever. Nor did it ever reoccur. Dr. Stewart said that I was healthy enough now to return to school for a half day, but I must remain indoors during recess. I did some makeup work during that time, but when my half day at school was done, I was to go home and rest in bed for a while. My parents arranged for my fourth grade teacher, and longtime family friend, to tutor me during the summer.

Eventually I was strong enough to stay for the entire school day and was allowed to go out with my classmates for recess. By this time, Dr. Stewart had given the okay for me to run and play. Our main recess activity was softball. No one wanted me on their team because I could never hit the ball past the pitcher's mound. It was agreed between the two teams that someone else would bat for me, and I would run the bases. What a thrill it was to be running again. I was beginning to feel that maybe I was a well person again.

Time passed and I was in high school. Dr. Stewart still kept a close watch on me. All these years since I had been so sick, he had insisted on my coming to his office if I caught a cold. One day, Mother noticed me sneezing and said that we better go to see the doctor. I replied that I really did not see the need to go to the doctor every time I had a cold. A very short time later, Mother and I were sitting in Dr. Stewart's office. When my name was called, I went back to one of the examining rooms. I repeated to Dr. Stewart what I had said to Mother. That was a mistake.

He slowly put my medical folder down on his desk, looked me in the eye, and said, "Young lady, let me tell you something. You nearly died when you were a little girl. It took a lot of medical knowledge on my part and a tremendous amount of care and attention on the part of your family to get you where you are today. Now I expect to see you in my office every time you sneeze. Do you understand me?"

I meekly replied, "Yes, sir."

He smiled and gave me a pat on my shoulder. Somehow I never felt it necessary to bring that topic up again.

Dr. Stewart continued to be our family doctor until I was nearly out of high school, at which time he relocated in another area.

I never did receive a certificate for perfect attendance.

I have enjoyed relatively healthy adult years. I am thankful that God spared my life. I am grateful that I had a very good family doctor and a loving, caring family. I was a very fortunate little girl. I appreciate my husband, Lee, who has watched over me throughout our nearly fifty years of marriage, always attentive in taking care of me. I had three normal, healthy children whom Lee and I raised. They, in turn, have given us six delightful grandchildren. I attended and graduated from college after our family grew up and left home. I taught school for ten years. I am now retired and get a joy from being church organist.

I am blessed that God has allowed me to lead a happy, productive life.

My Diary Key

Late one evening, I was in my bedroom looking for my diary key. My sister, Cheryl, aged three, copied every move I made and was my constant shadow.

After searching through all my dresser drawers, I decided to look in some boxes in my clothes closet. This closet was rather large. You could walk in and have ample room to move around. On one side, shelves were spaced from floor to ceiling. On the other side, there were some shelves then above that was a rod for hanging up clothes. I took a box from one of the shelves and began searching through it. Almost immediately, I saw the key. Just as I reached for it, everything went black, and I heard the closet door close. I pushed on the door, but it did not budge. It was shut tight. It would have been a simple matter to simply run my hand down the edge of the door until I felt the door knob. I deeply regretted the fact that the door had only one knob, and it was on the other side. I heard sounds coming from my bedroom, so I listened.

I could hear Cheryl on the other side of the door. She was singing in a very happy-sounding voice. I called out for her to open the door. She just gave me this bubbly chuckle and continued singing. I shifted around, so I could bend down and get my head on the closet floor. The door lacked a couple of inches touching the floor, so looking under the small space, I saw one of Cheryl's legs as she sat on the floor, rocking back and forth while continuing to sing.

I realized that she was going to be absolutely no help whatsoever. I heard Mother playing the piano. I could also hear Gabriel Heater sounding forth with the evening news. I decided to try to overpower

Cheryl's singing, Mother's playing, and the radio newscast. Drawing a deep breath, I hollered out where I was. No one heard me. After several tries, I spoke to Cheryl again, telling her to open the door. All I got back was more of her singing. I wondered how long it would be until supper.

It seemed like quite a long while before I noticed the piano music had stopped. Shortly after, I heard the door open and Mother told me supper was ready. I asked her when they discovered that I was missing. She replied that when the rest of the family came to the table, everyone (except Cheryl) asked, "Where is Linda?" Cheryl informed them that I was in the closet and could not get out because the door was shut.

From that day forth, any time I went into my closet, I made sure that Cheryl was nowhere nearby, and for safe measure, I put something heavy in the doorway.

A Special Blessing

I stood on the front porch and waved until the car was out of sight. I remained there for a few more minutes, aware of the awful feeling in the pit of my stomach, a feeling that I would never again see my mother alive. I was seventeen years old and a senior in high school, but I was scared. My parents, Charles and Opal Borders, were on their way to Ft. Smith, where Mother would have surgery. She had a place on her left arm that had become infected and must be removed. She said that the surgeon would do a little more while he was at it.

Mother did not want to have the surgery at this time for a special reason. I would be giving my senior music recital in a couple of weeks. For as long as I could remember, Mother talked of my recital. She and my music teacher, "Deedie," had worked together in the planning. Sometimes Mother would hear a piece of music and remark, "That would be a pretty selection for you to use." I had memorized pieces for voice, piano, and organ, which would provide a program of one and a half hours. When Mother spoke of this to the surgeon, he said that she could not delay the operation. He did assure her that she would be up and about in two weeks and able to attend my recital. With this assurance, Mother agreed. She told me this in such a way that I did not become overly concerned until I stood on the porch as they drove away. Memories of Mother drifted through my mind, carrying me on a journey into the past.

Any time I had gone to Mother with a problem, she always listened and offered a solution. When something happened in our community, whether it was funny, sad, or just an everyday event, my first thought was to share it with Mother. She was the focal point in my life.

Mother was called a ray of sunshine by her friends because of her happy disposition and willingness to help others when they were in need. She served in many different capacities of church work over the years. She enjoyed being a member of the Harmony Club, the Literary Club, Eastern Star, and Rotary Anns. Everyone always looked forward to Mother's programs. Any time she had meetings at our house, she would save a plate of the refreshments for Jennings, a lady who had worked for our family for many years. In fact, she was more like a member of the family than one who worked for us. Every time I was on one of Mother's programs, she would write me a thank-you note, expressing her appreciation.

One time, Mother and a friend of hers, Agnes, went to see the movie, *The Long, Long Trailer.* When the show was over, they returned to the house. I asked how they enjoyed it.

Agnes started laughing and said, "I can't tell you much about the movie. I laughed all the way through it, but it was not because of what I saw on the screen. I got so tickled watching your mother laugh. She can tell you about the show."

They both agreed that it was a very funny movie, and they enjoyed it immensely.

Music was an important part of Mother's life. She got a lot of pleasure from playing the piano and did it quite well. We had a console record player, which played records of 78 and 33 RPMs. The console cabinet contained record albums of the "big bands" of that era. There were also a number of records of classical music which Mother would play as she did her housework.

Getting ready for Sunday School every week was quite an interesting time at our house. Daddy, my younger sister Cheryl, and I would be ready and waiting on Mother. Daddy would walk around in the living room until he could stand it no longer. Then he would go into their bedroom finding Mother with a plain, unadorned hat in her hand. On the bed would be boxes of felt, lace, ribbon, and veiling. As Mother worked creating a new hat, Daddy would ask how much longer it was going to take her to get that hat finished. She would tell him that it would take her only a few minutes more, which meant we were most likely going to be late for Sunday School.

Mother was not casual about being tardy. I am sure that if the hat had not been in *Vogue*, we would have been on time every Sunday.

From the living room, I could hear the conversation and knew exactly what was coming next.

Daddy would ask, "Hon, why can't you make your hat on Friday or Saturday?"

Smiling, Mother would give him the most surprised look and reply, "Why, dear, I have no idea on either of those days what I am going to wear."

And that took care of that until the next Sunday when the entire episode would be repeated. I often thought that Mother should design hats because she always received many compliments on her millinery creations.

One after another, the amusing or happy memories drifted through my mind until suddenly, I was brought back to the present with a jolt and became very conscious of that awful feeling I had about Mother.

With a heavy heart, I went into the house. The total silence made me even more aware of my feelings. I tidied up the kitchen, hung up a few things in my bedroom, and then walked into the living room. I vacuumed the carpet, polished the furniture, and tried to practice my music, but I was too restless. I needed company.

I called a friend and classmate, "Nugget," and explained my reason for calling. I asked her if she could come over and be with me for a while. She said that she would be over in just a few minutes. Since we lived only six blocks apart, she was at my house almost before I hung up the phone. I made each of us a glass of iced tea, and we sat on the swing on the front porch while we talked.

We discussed a number of different topics. I am sure that Nugget was trying to get my mind off of Mother's surgery, but I am afraid she was not very successful. When it came time for her to go home, she asked me to call her when I heard from Daddy. She assured me that she would come over again anytime if I needed her. I thanked her and promised that I would call when I knew anything.

I went through the house to be sure everything was turned off then drove two blocks to Pappaw and Mammaw's house where they had moved to a few years earlier. As I entered the house, Mammaw was in the kitchen preparing lunch. I set the table and went into the living room to get Cheryl. The rest of the day passed slowly. Then the phone rang.

Mammaw answered it. I could tell that she was talking to Daddy. I was eager for her to hang up, so I could find out something about Mother.

At last, she ended the conversation, turned to me, and said, "Your mother has come out of surgery and is resting. Everything went well, they believe."

It was now time for me to think about what I would wear on my date with Lee, a young man I had been dating for nine months. We loved each other very much and planned to get married when I graduated from high school. Lee would be arriving that evening for the weekend. He always stayed with my aunt and uncle, who lived a short distance from my grandparent's house.

Lee arrived, and we went on our date but returned to my grandparent's house earlier than usual. I wanted to find out if Daddy had called again. He had not, so I assumed that Mother was doing okay. Even so, when Lee left and I began getting ready for bed, that uncertain feeling was there. Sleep did not come for several hours.

Saturday morning, I met our church organist, Ramona, at the church, so we could go over my solo for the next day, which would be Easter. After we finished, two other ladies came to the church, and we went over a hymn which we would sing as a trio for the Sunday evening worship service. After going over it a couple of times, we felt that we had it ready. Ramona locked the church, and we each went our own way. I had several errands to run for Mammaw. Then I stopped by the house to get what Cheryl and I would need for church on Sunday, making sure to get our new Easter frocks. Gathering all our things together, I carried them to the car and went to my grandparent's house.

As I put our things away, I asked Mammaw if Daddy had called. He had not. I helped Mammaw do some things around the house. Finally supper time arrived. Just as we sat down to eat, the phone rang. Daddy was calling to tell us that Mother was very uncomfortable, but the doctor said that she was doing okay. I asked him if he thought it a good idea for Lee to drive all of us up on Sunday afternoon for a quick visit. Daddy said that Mother wanted us to stay at home because it would be too much of a rush trip to come up there, and she said that we could visit when she returned home in a few days. We finished the phone call then sat down to eat. I hurried, so I could get ready for my date with Lee.

Lee arrived at the front door right on time, and we left to go to the movies. We returned home earlier than usual that night also. When I asked about Mother, Mammaw said that Daddy had not called. After a little while, Lee left for my aunt and uncle's house. I got ready for bed then made a quick check to be sure that Cheryl and I had everything we needed for church in the morning. I read a book for quite a while after getting in bed. Sleep was not going to come easy. Even as I dozed off, I was aware of that awful feeling in the pit of my stomach.

Sunday morning came, and I went over my song once before leaving for church. Lee met me at the church for the worship service. When it came time for the special music, I let the choir loft and walked to the pulpit. I noticed that the auditorium was full, and it seemed that every lady was wearing a new frilly hat. I thought of Mother and knew if she had been there, she would be wearing a cute, perky hat that she had fixed up, causing us to be late as usual. I missed her not being in the audience. She always smiled at me when I was singing for church or on a club program. Her warm assuring smile never failed to give me confidence.

After church, Lee went with me to my grandparent's house for Sunday dinner. Mammaw was a very good cook, and we had a delicious meal. Lee and Pappaw watched television while Mammaw and I cleaned up the kitchen, then we joined them in the living room.

The afternoon passed quickly, and too soon, it was time for me to take Lee to the train station, so he could return to work near Shreveport. Just as we were leaving, the phone rang. It was Daddy. He said that Mother was not feeling well. Her blood pressure was dropping, but the nurses were keeping a close watch on her. I asked Daddy if he wanted us to come to Ft. Smith.

He replied, "No, Mother and I want you to go on to church. I will call you later this evening."

As Lee and I got ready to go, I told Mammaw and Pappaw that as soon as Lee left on the train, I would go on to church.

I felt very restless all during the evening worship service and did not have my mind on the music when it came time for our trio to sing. We got through the song just fine, but I was relieved when we were finished and sat down. When the service was over, I saw a cousin of mine standing in the hall near the choir room. I could tell by the look on his face that the news was not good. He walked up to me and said that we needed to go straight to my grandparent's house. They had received a call from Daddy saying that we needed to come quickly to Ft. Smith. Mother had begun hemorrhaging, and they could not get it stopped.

When I arrived at my grandparent's house a few minutes later, they were ready to go. A family friend, Walter, was there to drive us. As we left their house, Mammaw asked me if I needed to stop by the house to get anything. I told her it would not be necessary. The awful feeling that I had experienced all weekend was now like a huge rock in the pit of my stomach. We rushed outside to the car and hurried on our way.

It was a dark night. Everyone in the car was quiet, each having their own thoughts and fears. We were nearing Y City when a state police car signaled for us to pull over. The officer, who had been given our car license number, walked to the driver's side of the car as Walter rolled down his window. The officer asked our destination, and Walter explained why we were on our way to Ft. Smith.

The officer then removed his hat and said, "The lady has died."

For several moments, there was total silence inside the car.

Then Cheryl asked Mammaw what the man was talking about. As a five-year-old, she sensed that something was wrong.

Then Pappaw remarked, "I just cannot understand how it happened so quickly."

Walter gave us a few minutes to compose ourselves, then he said to Pappaw, "What do you folks want to do? I will drive you on to Ft. Smith if that is what you want."

Pappaw and I had noticed that Mammaw was not doing well at all. She was short of breath, and even in the dim light inside the car, I could see how pale she was.

I looked at Pappaw and said, "I think we should return to Mena."

Pappaw asked, "What about Charles? How will he get home?"

Walter spoke up and said, "I am sure that folks are already learning about Opal's passing away. There will be friends who will go and bring Charles back to Mena."

With that, Pappaw said that we would return home. The officer expressed his sympathy and asked if he could be of any assistance. Walter thanked him and said that we would be okay. It was a slow, sorrowful return trip.

As we neared Mena, Pappaw asked Walter to stop at the home of Dr. Williams, Mammaw's doctor. Pappaw felt that she needed some medical attention. A few minutes later, Walter stopped the car at the doctor's house and went to the front door. He and the doctor had a brief conversation, and Walter returned to the car where we were waiting.

As he got in, he said, "The doctor told me that he would be at your house in just a few minutes."

We went two blocks further to my grandparent's house. As we got out of the car, I noticed that already there were a number of cars there. Friends had begun to come, and their presence made our homecoming easier. Even before we got in the house, we were told that two couples, who were close friends of Mother and Daddy, Murray and Agnes Johnson and Bert and Ramona Hensley, had left for Ft. Smith to bring Daddy back home. As we went into the house, the doctor arrived. Pappaw and I got Mammaw in bed and waited as the doctor examined her. He gave her something to help her relax. Then he sat by the bed for a couple of hours, watching closely. A friend of mine called the Mena depot and asked the agent to send a message to Shreveport for Lee. Friends kept coming in until the house was full. There was the sound of soft muffled voices expressing shock and sorrow. It was going to be a long night. Walter spent a few minutes with Pappaw and Mammaw before he left to go home. Pappaw thanked him for driving us.

Lee received my message immediately upon arriving in Shreveport. He called and told me that he would be on the next train coming to Mena. Some friends of mine said that they would go to the depot and pick him up when his train came in. Lee did arrive in the wee hours of the morning. It was a great comfort to me to have him there.

The next few days were a blur. People continued to come and go. Foods and flowers were in abundance. It was raining on the day of Mother's funeral, but the church was full. There had been so many orders for flowers that the florist shops in Mena ran out of flowers and had to order more from Texarkana. When all the space in the church was used up with sprays and arrangements of flowers, the shops notified Daddy that there were enough unfilled orders to last a year if they filled an order every Sunday. Daddy told them to go ahead with that plan and asked if they would, each Sunday after church, take the flowers to the hospital or the nursing home, which they agreed to do.

We tried to adjust to the drastic change in our lives. A few weeks later, I did give my senior music recital at our church and dedicated it to Mother's memory. After my high school graduation, Lee and I were married. Daddy sold our house, and he and Cheryl moved in with Pappaw and Mammaw.

Many times, I would think of telling Mother something, only to remember that I could no longer share things with her. So very often, I would see someone at church or in town, and they would have a story about Mother that they wanted to share with me. We would have never known about the many times Mother had helped people in their time of need if they had not shared their stories with us. Time went on, but always, there were a number of people telling me how much they had thought of Mother.

Years passed. Lee and I reared our family of three children— Dawn, Brian, and Susan. They grew up and left home to start their own families. Still, there were people who remembered with fondness something about Mother. Over a period of time, things changed.

I had to remind myself that it had been a long time since Mother's death. Nearly all the people she had worked with in church and the different organizations had passed on. There was hardly any left that knew her really well. I began to feel that I was the only one left who thought of her. Now there was no one who knew what Mother was like with whom I could share a funny or heartwarming story. I missed that.

I always thought about her but especially on her birthday and the date she died, April 10. Then one Sunday morning, an incident occurred at church, the same church where I had grown up and now served as an organist. I had my choir robe on and was waiting until it was time for me to go into the auditorium to begin playing the prelude music. A number of people came by on their way from Sunday School to the sanctuary for the worship service. As they passed by, we would exchange brief conversations.

One lady, Louise Drye, paused and said, "I had a phone call from Becky the other day."

I knew Becky Wallace and her family from the time they had lived in Mena. Becky had lived in Ft. Smith now for a number of years but continued to be interested in the people she had known in Mena.

Louise continued with our conversation by saying, "She always asks about you. I told her that you were doing fine. Then Becky told me that she thought of Opal the other day."

I looked surprised and said, "My goodness, what made her think of Mother?"

Louise looked at me and smiled. Then she said, "Linda, Becky and I think of your mother especially on the tenth of April. We call each other often, and one of us will mention Opal. We have not missed a year thinking of her on that date."

I stood there almost as if I was frozen in place.

After a moment, I said to Louise, "How sweet of both of you to remember Mother throughout all these years. Louise, do you realize that it has been fifty years since Mother died? You have no idea how much it means to me to know that the two of you think of her on that date. I had begun to feel that I was the only one left who thought of her at any time, much less on that particular date. Thank you so much for sharing that with me."

Louise replied, "Your mother was a very special lady."

I smiled as I walked to the organ. I felt a warm, comforting feeling in my heart as I thought, *Thank You, Lord, for the wonderful Mother that You gave me. I am thankful that on this day You gave me a special blessing of knowing that others still remember Mother with fondness.*

Dawn

When we lived in Pittsburg, Kansas on Olive Street, while Lee was working on the Kansas City Southern Railroad, we lived in a three-story house that had been converted into apartments. We lived in one of the two apartments on the ground floor.

The day we moved in, the older lady living in the other ground floor apartment came down the hall to welcome us. Lee and I smiled, introduced ourselves, and invited her to come in.

Lee took a second look at her and asked, "Did you say your last name is Carr?"

She smiled and said, "Yes, and I think I know you."

She affirmed that she and Lee had lived in the same small town a few years back.

Lee said, "I remember that you had a lot of cats."

Mrs. Carr smiled and replied that the cats numbered twenty-seven. She would take in any stray or unwanted cat and was known in that town for giving each of them a good home where they received loving care. We had a delightful visit, and Mrs. Carr was especially taken with our two-year-old daughter, Dawn. Often, Dawn wanted to go and see "Carr." I would open our door and watch until she knocked on Mrs. Carr's door. Her door would open, and I always heard her say, "Well, hello, come in." After a while, I would go and visit a moment before Dawn and I returned to our apartment.

We lived there several months before the railroad sent us to another location. One day, we received a letter from Mrs. Carr. Enclosed was a poem she had written as follows:

Dawn

You are a tiny little girl, for you are only two,
I know your mommy and daddy are very proud
of you.

I miss you very much, and wish that you were here,
It was always a pleasure to know that you were
near.

I miss you knocking on my door,
I miss you playing on my floor.

The thing I miss the most by far,
Is the little girl who called me "Carr."

We learned that Carr passed away a few years later.

While living in that apartment, we became acquainted with the couple living next door named Cordray. We visited with them often, and even after we moved away, we kept in touch. We enjoyed returning to Pittsburg a number of times for a visit, and they traveled to our town to see us. It was always a delight to see them.

"Dawn".
you are a tiny little girl
for you are only two,
I know that Mommie and Daddy
are very proud of you.

I miss you very very much
and wish that you were here,
it always was a pleasure
to know that you were near.
I miss you knocking on my door,
I miss you playing on my floor,
the thing I miss the most by far,
is the little girl who called me "Car".

Mrs. Carr lived next to us in Pittsburg, Kansas, where we lived on Olive
St. She had lived in Anderson, and she and Lee knew each other.
Later we lived on Locust Ave., and the picture was taken there

Olive St. your first birthday. You had a lovely party.

Brian and My Special Gift

On a lovely summer day when you were three years old, you were having a grand time playing in the yard. I needed to be doing some work in the house, but you were having such a good time.

I walked around picking up small twigs and tossing them over the fence into our back field. You seemed to be looking for something, so I searched every nook and cranny only to come up empty-handed. I walked here and there, waiting for you to decide to pursue some other adventure when suddenly I heard the telephone ringing.

Running into the house, I kept a close watch on you through the window as I answered the phone. It was a friend calling, and I explained to her that you were outside and that I would call her back a little later. Just as I hung up the phone, it rang again. I quickly answered and repeated the same explanation and placed the phone receiver back in place. As I started outside, I saw you coming to the house. As you approached me, you were smiling, and your eyes just sparkled. You reached out your hand and presented me with a beautiful small bouquet of wildflowers you had picked.

I took the flowers and said, "Brian, these flowers are so colorful. They look like they came from the flower shop."

Bending over, I gave you a hug and remarked how lovely they were. Then I suggested that we go in the house and find a vase for them and give them some water. You agreed, and in the house, I searched for a small vase that would show off the colors. Not finding anything suitable, I remembered that I had tossed a large-sized empty bottle of vanilla extract in the trash earlier that day. I retrieved the bottle and washed it really good on the outside and rinsed it thoroughly inside. I put water in it and then hoped each tiny stem would

74

fit in the opening. With a sigh of relief, the last flower eased into place. I found a tiny doily and placed it and the vase on a small table in the living room. You had watched me from the time we entered the house until now, and I asked you how it looked, and you said that you liked it.

I saved that bottle and used it a number of times for the flowers you brought to me, but that first lovely bouquet was a *special gift*.

My First Experience with Country Living

When Lee and I were married in 1955, his job with the Signal Corp of a railroad kept us on the move. In fact, we moved fifty-four times in seven years. The Corp installed railroad crossing signals and train signals. Normally, it took the Corp two to three weeks to complete a job, then we were sent on to another assignment for the railroad. For the last four of those seven years, we had our own house trailer. It was eight feet wide and thirty-two feet long. We enjoyed the trailer because it was so much nicer having our house with us everywhere we went, instead of spending hours looking at apartments. The trailer provided comfortable living for Lee and I and our daughter, Dawn, who was age two when we got the trailer.

In 1959, our second child, Brian, was born. The four of us were still comfortable in our trailer. The children's bedroom was equipped with bunk beds. Lee built a side rail for the lower bunk to make it safe for Brian.

In 1962, Dawn was six and would enter the first grade in September. That was going to be a busy month because our third child was due on September 5. Lee and I knew we could not change Dawn from school to school, so we decided that it was necessary for the children and I to settle down in my hometown, Mena.

My grandmother wanted us to stay with her until after the baby came. Our family doctor told me to be back in Mena absolutely no later than the last part of August. During the final week of August, Lee moved the children and I to my grandmother's house. I did not like the idea of our family being separated, but for the present time, it could not be helped.

I got Dawn enrolled in school just before Susan arrived on September 4, weighing eight pounds, seven ounces. After a few weeks with my grandmother, the children and I moved back into the trailer. Having a new baby and all the things they require really made our trailer crowded. Lee built a one-room addition to the trailer. It helped a lot, but we still needed more space. Lee and I began talking about finding a house.

Lee had to do most of the inquiring and looking at houses as I was taking care of the sick children. Dawn had come down with a serious case of chicken pox. Right on schedule, Brian got the pox from Dawn. Just as his spots were beginning to fade, Susan got the pox. She was only six months old at the time, and she could not understand that she must not scratch her itchy places. I kept a pair of socks on her hands to prevent her scratching the sore places and making them worse.

Finally the children recovered. Lee took us to look at several places. One house we were considering was in the country. I had strong reservations about this house as I had grown up in town. Lee, on the other hand, had spent a part of his growing-up years on a farm. There was one big plus influencing us to take the house. The retired couple owning it wanted a smaller place to keep up. In fact, they were looking at house trailers and were very pleased with the design and size of ours. This made an ideal arrangement for us since we had not acquired any furniture or appliances, and they did not want to take any furniture with them into a trailer.

For me, there was one big minus in taking the house. I knew nothing about a water well and pump, a vegetable garden, chickens, and ground rattlers.

I comforted myself by thinking, *Oh well, if we decide to take the house, Lee will be able to solve any problems that arise.*

We did buy the house, but little did I know that seldom would a problem present itself on a weekend when Lee would be home.

The house was an old one. It had been built with no subfloors or insulation. At some time in the past, former owners had made two additions to the house. These additions were not made by skilled carpenters as was evidenced by an unlevel floor in one of the rooms. The dining room was on the north side of the house, and the windows framed a beautiful mountain scene. There would be many times later that I would pause at the windows to admire the view thinking what a lovely room it was. I would continue to think of the dining room as a pleasant part of the house until a couple of months after we moved in, and the cold north wind began blowing. When the wind blew, the windows whistled and rattled. The curtains had a gentle ripple as plenty of fresh air entered the room. When a cold wind blew, the children and I went into the living room to have our meals near the heater. For now, my thoughts were of getting our things ready to move.

Since Lee was only home on weekends, we moved on a Saturday. It was on Susan's first birthday. Even amid the hectic day, I got a picture of her and her birthday cake adorned with one candle.

We carried packed boxes into the house and unpacked some of them. Dawn and Brian helped by carrying in some small boxes. From time to time, I noticed that Susan would take something out of a packed box.

I thought, *I know where she is, she is content, and what she has cannot hurt her.* So I went on with my tasks.

I was to regret those thoughts later. For the next few weeks, I found "missing" items in the most unlikely places. At first, I was puzzled as to how they got in such an unusual location. Then it slowly dawned on me that at the tender age of one, Susan had become an accomplished pack rat.

Moving day was a long tiring one. By bedtime, we had a clear path through the house and a stack of empty boxes on the back porch. With the children in bed sound asleep, Lee and I soon collapsed into our bed.

The next morning came at least six hours too early. Lee and I were awakened by the squawking of twenty-eight chickens. It seemed we forgot to feed them the day before, and they were not happy. Knowing that any more sleep was out of the question, Lee bounded out of bed and headed toward the bathroom. Since my side of the bed was against the wall, I had to scoot to get to the edge of the bed. One short scoot brought me to a quick stop. Every inch of me was sore. It took me considerable more time than usual to get out of bed.

Once I was standing on the floor, I thought, *I do not want to move anything. I think I will just fall backward onto the bed, pull the cover over my head, and be very still.*

It was a lovely thought, but the children would be waking up any minute, so I slowly made my way to the kitchen to prepare breakfast.

I thought that cold cereal would be nice, but then I remembered that there was a wire basket full of fresh eggs in the refrigerator. Unless I missed my guess, there would be more eggs to gather that day, so I decided on fried eggs for breakfast.

I dug around in the packed boxes until I found the cast-iron griddle. I greased it and placed it on a lit burner. I got the eggs from the refrigerator and sat them on a side table. The coffee was brewing, the milk was poured in the children's glasses, and the table was set. I was ready to start frying eggs. I took an egg from the wire basket, cracked the shell, and eased the egg onto the griddle. Immediately, I turned and got a second egg from the basket. I broke that shell and started to drop the egg onto the griddle when my hand stopped in midair. I looked at the griddle. The egg was gone.

I stood there and thought, *I know I am tired, and my mind has been racing ahead to think of all we need to do today before Lee has to board the train to go to work, but I know I put an egg on that griddle.*

Oh well, no matter, time was wasting. We would need to be getting ready for Sunday School and church before long. I dropped the second egg from its shell onto the griddle. As I reached for the third egg, I took a quick sideways glance at the griddle. It was empty.

Okay, I thought, *that's enough.*

I turned off the burner. I was going to find the eggs that had disappeared.

Lee came into the kitchen and asked, "Where's breakfast?"

I replied, "I don't know. I can't find it." He had a puzzled look on his face as I exclaimed, "There they are!"

Lee looked in the direction I was pointing. Sure enough, there were the two missing eggs, on the floor, clear across the room. Those eggs had slid off the griddle and continued to slide across the unlevel floor. I do not know what would have happened to cold storage eggs, but these were farm fresh eggs. The whites were as firm as Jell-O. The deep orange–colored yolks were just as firm. I scooped up the eggs and trashed them. It was at this moment that I decided cold cereal would be nice for breakfast. At least in the dining room, we could keep the milk in the cereal bowls.

Lee leveled the stove that day before the children and I took him to town to board the train for work. He tested his efforts by telling me to fry an egg on the griddle. It stayed put. Several weeks later, he leveled the kitchen floor.

During the years that we lived in the house in the country, I prepared fried eggs a number of times. I always chuckled at that first attempt to fry eggs when they had suddenly disappeared. I would have many more unique experiences during the period we lived at this place.

My Lipstick

I picked up the ringing telephone and said hello. I stood there, frozen, as I learned that my father had suffered a heart attack. He was in a hospital and was, at the moment, stable. I immediately began making preparations to go to him.

I called Mammaw, and explained about the telephone call I had received. I asked her if she could keep the children while I was gone. It would mean that she would have to drive them to school and pick them up each day in addition to cooking and taking care of them. Of course, they were big enough to help her do some things which would make it easier for her. She said for me to make my plans to go. She would be happy to keep them with her. I talked to the children, explaining why they would be staying with Mammaw for a few days while I went to see how my father was doing. The children called him Big Daddy, and they were concerned about him too.

For the children to stay with Mammaw was no problem for them at all. They always enjoyed going to her house, and since she lived just a few miles from us, we saw her often. I let them pack what they wanted to take with them—favorite pillows, books, and games. I told them that I would return on Friday.

I packed their clothes and other things they would need. As I drove them to Mammaw's house, I admonished each one to be helpful while there and to be on their best behavior. After we got all of their things in Mammaw's house, I gave them hugs and said my goodbyes. Then I drove to the train station.

I boarded the train in Mena and made the trip to Galena Park and immediately went to the hospital. I could hardly wait to see Daddy. He had been told that I was coming, so it would not be a surprise when I walked into his room.

There were flowers all around and cards on the bed stand. He looked a little pale but said that he felt pretty good. The nurses told me later that he kept them laughing. I spent a good part of each day with him.

One day while I was sitting in his hospital room, I asked him what changes the doctor said he would have to make in his lifestyle.

Daddy replied, "No more smoking or coffee, cut back on the peanut butter, and get to bed earlier, or expect a more damaging heart attack in the future."

I remarked, "I don't see a problem with any of that except the peanut better."

We had a laugh.

All through my growing-up years, Daddy and I had met in the kitchen at bedtime, where both of us enjoyed a peanut butter sandwich, or we would each take a banana and put peanut butter on them. It was a long-standing habit that would be hard to break.

Before I knew it, the week was gone. Daddy was feeling much better, and his doctor said that he would be going home in a day or two. On my last visit to his hospital room, I admonished him to do what the doctor said. His vague response made me doubt how serious he was taking his condition. I reminded him that during my childhood when I was sick so many times, he had told me that we must do what the doctor said. Now it was time for him to do as the doctor said. The next day, family members took me to the train station, and I left for home.

As the train pulled out of the station, my thoughts went ahead to when I would arrive in Shreveport, Louisiana, where I would have to change trains. He was working near Shreveport at a place where it was very difficult to get word to him, so I had decided when I left Mena on Monday, to surprise him on Friday by appearing on the train platform.

All the long way to Shreveport, I imagined the different ways he would respond to seeing me there at the train station. I almost chuckled out loud several times thinking of the look that would be on his face. Part of the time I tried to read a book, or look out of the window, but nothing occupied my thoughts like the anticipation of surprising Lee.

Finally the conductor announced that we were approaching Shreveport. I gathered my things and anxiously waited while the train shuffled around and backed into the station.

My goodness, I thought, *they could have done all of that after we got off the train.*

There were quite a few people ahead of me, but eventually, I stepped off the train and started walking down the long platform to the station. After only a moment, I saw Lee and many others of the Signal Corp outside the station waiting for the train. Lee was seated on one of the benches along with others of the corp. Some of the men were standing behind the benches. A couple of the men standing behind Lee recognized me and waved. They kept looking at Lee as I waved back.

I thought, *Lee is going to jump up and run to meet me just any second now.*

It did not happen. I kept walking down the platform carrying my suitcase. With every step, I kept my eyes on Lee, knowing that he would move toward me at any time. I walked on and on. By this time, I was getting upset. I was mindful that none of the imagined greeting I had envisioned were happening. He just continued to sit there and look and me. What was the matter with him anyhow? Besides, that suitcase was heavy, and my high heels did not help matters any. Some of the men were having a very hard time keeping their amusement to themselves. I saw several of them cover their mouths or turn aside. Well, I was not amused. I was quite put out. Finally I walked right up to him. He continued to look at me but said not a word.

Some of the men just could not hold their laughter in any longer as I spoke to Lee, saying, "Well, aren't you even going to speak?"

He just sat there very nonchalantly and remarked, "I thought to myself, That woman sure looks like my wife. She is the same size as my wife, and she even walks like my wife. But that lady isn't wearing lipstick, and my wife never goes anywhere without putting on lipstick. So it can't be my wife."

Some of the men said, "Yeah, he just didn't want to carry your suitcase."

Everyone but me had a chuckle over the incident. That was the first I had thought about lipstick. I had been so excited about surprising Lee that, for once, putting on my lipstick never occurred to me.

About that time, our train arrived at the station, and we all boarded it. It took me a little while to get back in a good mood, but I promised myself that I would never be caught again without lipstick on. We continued the journey to Mena. Arriving there, Lee and I went to Mammaw's house and picked up the children, then we made our way to our house.

A few days later, Daddy did get to go home from the hospital. He continued to keep his forbidden habits. All of us in the family lovingly scolded him from time to time. Eight years later, he died from a massive heart attack at the age of fifty-two.

Pickles

My first attempt at making pickles was a unique experience.

When we moved to a house in the country, a large, productive vegetable garden came with the property.

Living in the country, gardening, processing the food, dealing with a water well pump, unruly hens, and ground rattlers were all new to me.

On a lovely, sunny day, I put on my wide-brimmed hat, picked up my basket, and headed for the garden. I would pick cucumbers today. I hoped there would be enough to start a batch for pickles.

When I looked under the leaf of one cucumber plant, I jumped. There was the biggest cucumber I had ever seen. I had just picked cucumbers two days ago. I looked around. There were cucumbers everywhere. How in the world did so many more cucumbers appear in such a short period of time? However, most of the cucumbers were gherkin sized, three to four inches long and less than an inch across.

Walking back to the house with the basketful of cucumbers, I reminded myself to call a longtime family friend to ask if she would share with me her recipe for sweet pickles. I had previously eaten some she had made, and they were very crisp and delicious.

A few moments later, I was talking to my friend on the phone, and she gladly shared her recipe.

Now I could get started. I found an earthenware crock in our basement. After cleaning it up, I washed the cucumbers and dumped them in the crock. I poured the brine of pickling salt dissolved in boiling water over the cucumbers. The cucumbers were kept in this solution for seven days and had to remain completely covered with the brine. I found a dinner plate that was a perfect fit in the crock, but a few cucumbers floated to the top of the brine. I needed something to keep the plate weighted down. I went outside and very soon found a suitable rock. I gave it a good scrubbing and placed it on the plate. No cucumbers popped up this time. I used a tea towel to cover the top of the crock.

When the time was up, I poured off the brine, washed the cucumbers, and because I was going to leave them whole, I used an ice pick to make a tiny hole in both ends of each cucumber.

Next I put the cucumbers back in the crock and poured an alum solution over them to make them crisp. This step took twenty-four hours.

The next day, I made the syrup. For three days, I heated the syrup and poured it over the pickles. On the third day, I packed the pickles into sterilized canning jars, poured the piping hot syrup over them, and sealed them. My pickling rock was saved and used year after year for pickle making.

I felt like a full-fledged gardener, sharing a bond with all those who had gone before me, producing and processing healthy, tasty foods for their families from their own gardens.

Finally the pickling process was complete, but before I packed the pickles, I eagerly sampled one. It did not taste like my friend's pickles, and they looked funny too. Well, I could not be worried about that now. I had a job to finish. Anyhow, maybe pickles needed a few days for the flavor to develop.

Proudly, I lined up the eight jars of pickles in a row on a side table in the kitchen. I stood there a moment to admire the results of my efforts. As I washed the crock and other utensils I had used in hot soapy water, the thought kept lingering in the back of my mind that those pickles just did not look right. I decided we would open the first jar when Lee came home that weekend from his job on the railroad. I could hardly wait for Lee to arrive home, so I could show him my achievement. In fact, I pondered the various ways he would shower me with his compliments and praise.

When Lee did arrive home, I was not prepared for his question as I proudly handed him one of the jars of pickles.

He slowly turned the jar around full circle and then asked, "Where are the bumps?"

I thought, *Bumps! Who would be interested in bumps when I had gone through eleven days of careful preparation to produce those quality pickles?*

While I was recovering from his question, not to mention the fact that there was a total lack of any praise or compliments on his part, he asked the same question again, "Where are the bumps? Pickles have small bumps on them. These are smooth."

It was very obvious that he was losing the struggle to keep a straight face, but he was trying. I could tell. He was trying.

Bumps indeed. With my hands on my hips, I retorted, "I peeled them."

As Lee turned to look at the other seven jars, I saw his shoulders shaking slightly. I might have thought that he was sobbing for some unexplained reason except for giggles that erupted.

He took several moments to gain his composure then said, "That must have been some task to peel one gallon of gherkin-sized cucumbers. Why did you peel them?"

Immediately mental pictures of pickles came to my mind. Pickles in jars, pickles in pretty little dishes served with a meal, pickles everywhere, and all of them had bumps on them. I was feeling very foolish.

With a low mumble, I replied, "I peel nearly everything I pick in the garden. Besides, I peel cucumbers that I put in a salad. I just thought I was supposed to peel cucumbers for pickles too."

Lee chuckled again and said, "I am sure they will be very tasty. Let's eat supper."

I called our two older children—Dawn, age seven, and Brian, age five—to come in and wash their hands for supper. Susan, age two, was right there, so I put her in the high chair.

I passed the newly opened pickles around the table along with the rest of the food. I noticed that everyone took one pickle. I was the first to bite into my pickle, and immediately, the rest of the family pushed their pickles over to the very edge of their plates. Nothing was said. I just stood up, got the pickles, and took them to the kitchen. As I returned to the dining table, I saw Lee take a tiny nibble from his pickle.

He coughed a couple of times, and his eyes watered, but his only comment was "Bit tart."

After we finished the meal, with recipe in hand, I called the lady who had given the recipe to me. I told her of the reaction both Lee and I had experienced when we sampled the pickles. I related to her how I had done each step of the pickling process.

She went straight to the cause of the problem by asking, "Linda, how much vinegar did you use?"

I replied, "Eight cups."

She assured me that this amount was correct. Then she asked, "How much sugar did you use?"

I answered, "One cup."

I heard a gasp, then she said, "I am sure I told you to use ten cups of sugar. Look at what you wrote down when I gave you the recipe several days ago."

I closely examined my copy of the recipe, and sure enough, there it was, a small, almost indivisible zero, which would make it ten cups.

She remarked, "I sure am sorry about your pickles, especially since this is not an inexpensive recipe, but you will have to throw them away."

Feeling I had lost any claim to call myself a gardener, I emptied all the pickles into a pail. I carried the pail outside and walked across our backyard. Dawn, Brian, and Susan were following close behind. As I approached the fence, I noticed our neighbor's thirty-year-old mule, Toby, grazing nearby. With a sigh, thinking of all that work that was wasted, I tossed the pickles over the fence. Toby loped over to investigate. He took one quick whiff and kicked both hind legs skyward. He galloped off at a gait that would have put a mule half his age to shame.

It took three days before Toby would venture over to that spot again.

In the following years, I won several blue ribbons at our county fair for my sweet pickles, but my first attempt at making pickles was a disaster.

Dedication Service

November 1, 1964

The day we dedicated our new church building is a time I will remember. I was especially excited because Daddy, my stepmother Lucille, and my sister Cheryl drove up from Galena Park, and I was looking forward to a good visit with them. There had been no opportunity to see them before church, but Daddy called me and said that they would have to slip out of church early in order to attend a funeral but that we would have a good lengthy visit later that afternoon.

It was time for church to begin. I was a choir member, and we were all lined up ready to go into our new auditorium. As we walked into the choir loft and sat down, I began looking around the congregation for my family. My, the auditorium was packed. We began singing the first hymn, and I continued looking around at the many faces. Even though I could only see the upper part of his face, I finally located Daddy. I smiled, and he gave a warm grin back. From time to time during the sermon, I would glance in Daddy's direction and smile. He always sent a wide smile back to me. The next time I looked his way, I smiled *and* winked. Something I would not have done if we had seen each other before church. There were several times during the remainder of the service that I looked at Daddy with a smile and a wink, and he would smile and wink back.

As our pastor neared the end of his sermon, it was time for Daddy, Lucille, and Cheryl to leave. As I watched, they stood up and quietly walked out from the other side of the auditorium! I never did find out who the man was that I shared smiles and winks with, but I never did that again.

The Pump

The house we lived in for several years had a water pump. At some time, the owners had added on to the house covering the pump, so it was necessary to crawl under the house when the pump needed attention. The well held a very small amount of water, so I had to schedule bath times, washing clothes and dishes.

One morning, I tried to run water in the kitchen sink to give one-year-old Susan, our youngest child, a bath. Well, the faucet was turned on full force, but not a drop of water came out. I went to the opening of the cellar and crawled in. I checked the few things I knew about the pump, and everything seemed okay, but we still had no water. Since Lee was away during the week, working on the Kansas City Southern Railroad, I called Uncle Harry and Aunt Mina, who lived a short distance from us, and told her about my problem. Aunt Mina said that they would be right over. A very short time later, they arrived. I walked with them to the back of the house where the opening was. Aunt Mina and I stood there and visited while Uncle Harry crawled under the house.

After a few minutes, Uncle Harry came out and said, "Linda, you have lost your prime."

I thought for a second and replied, "Uncle Harry, I don't think so because I haven't taken anything off of the pump."

He looked at me, and with a cigar whirling round and round in his mouth, he asked, "What in the whole world are you doing living in the country? I've known you all of your life, and you and your family have always lived in town."

I looked at him and replied, "Believe me, I have asked myself that same question many times each day."

They both looked at me and grinned.

I walked over to the neighbor's house and got some water, carried it back, and handed it to Uncle Harry. He took it and went back under the house again. Very soon, he came out and walked over to where Aunt Mina and I were standing.

He said, "Now go in the house and turn on the water. See if you have a good stream flowing."

I hurried to the kitchen and turned the faucet on. Oh, the delight to see that water gushing out. I turned the water off and rushed outside to tell Uncle Harry and Aunt Mina that all was well (no pun intended).

I invited them to come in, but they said they needed to get back home. I gave Susan her bath and felt grateful for Uncle Harry's help.

When Lee got home that weekend, I told him what had happened. He drove over to another neighbor's house and asked him if he would come over to our house and pick a good spot for us to have the well drilled. He said he would be over that afternoon. When he showed up, he had a long stick in his hand. We watched as he walked around the yard with that stick still in his hand. Suddenly we saw that stick point downward. I was watching him the whole time, and that stick did move.

The neighbor, whose name also was Lee, said, "This is the spot you need to have the well drilled."

My Lee contacted a well drilling company, and very soon, we had the well drilled, *and* there was a tremendous amount of water available. I joyfully tore up the schedule of when-to-do chores that required water. I could now use water to my heart's delight!

At Eddard's Swimming Hole

During the twenty-six years that Lee worked at the post office, he had Mondays off, so on a hot summer Monday, we decided to take the boat and drive the short distance from our house to Eddard's Hole for a relaxing time. We could cool off in the water then get in the boat and row down the river. I told Dawn and Brian to get into their swimming gear. Susan was still a little tot and not knowing how to swim yet; Lee and I secured her in a new life jacket. Soon we were on our way, going down the dusty country road and looking forward to getting to the river.

Splash into the water we went. Dawn and Brian had a delightful time playing and enjoying the cool, flowing water. Lee and I held onto Susan even though she had the protection of the life jacket. After a while, Lee got the boat down to the edge of the water and held onto it as we stepped in and sat down. We just sat there for a few moments under the shade of tree branches that extended over the edge of the water, enjoying the breeze that felt cool on our wet skin.

Suddenly I exclaimed, "Lee, let's get out of here!"

He replied, "Okay, in just a minute."

I immediately stated, "If that snake on the branch over my head decides to drop down into this boat—"

I never had a chance to finish my statement. Lee had grabbed the oars and was rowing like he was in a speed race. Very quickly, we were out from under those tree branches, and all was safe but not yet calm. Dawn and Brian looked like they had swallowed a big wad of gum. I was just waiting for my heart to stop pounding. Susan, with her arm over the edge of the boat, was totally absorbed in watching her hand make ripples in the water as Lee guided the boat along.

Then with a gasp, I screamed, "Lee! Susan is in the river!"

All I could see was her life jacket. She had slipped over the edge of the boat and was underwater. In a flash, Lee reached over and grabbed the life jacket with a firm hand and lifted her out of the water and into the boat. When he saw that she was breathing okay, he hugged her and gave me her hand. We both thanked God for saving her. Lee rowed us back to shore, and by the way, that snake had moved. We carefully got out of the boat and onto dry land.

Lee said, "I think we are ready to go home."

Dawn, Brian, and I eagerly agreed. Susan was still a bit shaken from her dip in the water.

Arriving home, Lee and I looked that life jacket over thoroughly and found that it was weighted wrong, which caused Susan's head to be thrust under the water. We took the life jacket out to our back field, away from the trees, and set it afire. We watched until it was completely burned up and thanked God again that we were all safe and back home.

The next day, we went to town to buy another life jacket for Susan. We told the salesman at the store what had happened the previous day. He took the jacket to a back room, being gone for several minutes.

Returning, he said, "This jacket is weighted correctly and is completely safe."

We thanked him, paid for the jacket, and went home. That life jacket was used many times and did what it was supposed to do— keep Susan's head out of the water. It contributed to a number of fun outings that were far more relaxing and enjoyable than that day at Eddard's Hole.

The Unusual Visit

As Mrs. Wilmont took me into her sunroom, I thought that it was the most inviting room I had ever been in. I felt like I could spend many pleasant hours there.

Just then, her telephone rang.

"Make yourself comfortable while I answer the telephone. I will be brief, then we can get started on the recipes you have compiled for our club cookbook." With that, she went into the hall.

As I entertained myself by looking around the room, there was something that I found very puzzling. While I pondered this, I looked at the center of the room. There was a hanging platform full of plants. It looked like an island of greenery. I noticed that the platform could be lowered when watering and maintenance were needed. There were a number of other plants placed in an attractive manner around the room. There was not a droopy leaf or wilted blossom on any of the plants. Mrs. Wilmont had something which I greatly lacked, a green thumb. I made a mental note to ask her how she cared for her plants.

I kept thinking about the part of the room that puzzled me as I continued to look around. Over in one corner was a walnut table with intricate carvings. It was adorned with a delicate ivory tablecloth that had elaborate handwork and matching napkins. I wondered if someone in Mrs. Wilmont's family had made the luncheon set years ago. There was a dainty tea set on the table, and I could smell the delicious aroma of apple berry tea steeping in the pot. Under a clear-glass dome cover, I saw a plate of sliced apricot almond bread. Also on the table, there were two place settings of china dessert plates with a rose pattern. The comfortable cane bottom chairs were of a design that I had not seen before. They were arranged so that whether there were two people or ten, there could be an easy flow of conversation. The lighting in the sunroom was recessed almost to the point of being invisible and was needed only on very overcast days and evenings.

My eyes wondered over to the glazed windows that went from ceiling to floor, giving the room its bright and airy atmosphere and offering a full view of a most colorful flower garden complete with a frequently used birdbath. I thought how restful it would be just to sit and enjoy the flowers and birds. The scene reminded me again of Mrs. Wilmont's green thumb.

Again, my mind went back to the puzzling part of the room, and I was still reflecting on this when I heard Mrs. Wilmont return.

"Well, I am sorry that I was longer on the telephone than I had thought. But now, I will pour us a cup of tea, and while we have some slices of bread with it, we will get to work on the recipes. Why don't we sort the recipes according to categories, like breads, beverages, cakes, meats, and so forth?"

I replied, "I think that is a good idea."

For the next little while, we were both busy getting the recipes in proper order. Then came a more difficult task. We had to go over every recipe word for word to look for several things—correct spelling, nothing left out, and clarity of directions. At long last, our job was finished. The recipes were ready for mailing to the company that would make the cookbooks for us.

As Mrs. Wilmont poured both of us a fresh cup of tea, she suggested that we just relax for a little while. I agreed. I could not resist the temptation to inquire about the part of the room which had puzzled me.

"This is a lovely room and so attractively arranged. I am sure you spend a lot of time here. If I had such a room as this in my house, I am sure it would be my favorite. I noticed the rocker over there in the corner. It has aroused my curiosity."

Mrs. Wilmont laughed and said, "Everyone asks me about that rocker. If you wish, I will be happy to tell you the story. However, I must warn you, it is not a story that can be told in a few minutes."

I replied, "That statement only sharpens my interest. I would love to hear your story."

Mrs. Wilmont said, "Make yourself comfortable. We are going on a journey."

I settled back in my chair, and with tea cup in hand, I looked forward to learning the history of the rocker.

Mrs. Wilmont began, "My father, Mr. Perryton Jr., gave me that rocker when Mr. Wilmont and I married nearly fifty years ago. I remembered it from my earliest youth and was delighted to have it in my home. As you have probably guessed, it is handmade. When my father gave it to me, I asked him where he got it. He told me that his father had given it to him when he and my mother were married. My grandfather did not make the rocker. His mother had handed it down to him on his wedding day. The story does not end there. As you may have noticed, each family member that received the rocker had it given to him or her on their wedding day."

I was eager to hear the rest of the story. Taking a sip of tea, I said, "Please go on. I am beginning to understand why you wanted the rocker in this room."

Mrs. Wilmont continued, "My great-grandfather, Tom Dowel, was married in 1879. He received the rocker from his father, James Dowel. James was married in 1859. The following year, he joined the confederacy to fight in the Civil War. Before he left home, he told his wife, Jane, that if the Yankee soldiers took over their place, she was to hide the rocker along with some other things they treasured. Sure enough, several months after James had left, a few Yankee soldiers rode into the yard. Jane did not have time to hide anything. They got some cured hams and food stuffs that they could carry with them. Jane sat down in the rocker and waited. There came a loud knock on the door. Jane told them to come in. She said that she would serve them something, but she was worn out from nursing a child, sick with smallpox. The soldiers could not get away fast enough, leaving the hams and food behind. The rocker survived the war as did James.

"Going farther back in time, when my ancestor, Peter Richards, fought in the Revolutionary War, he left his wife, Elizabeth, and six children behind at the home place.

"One day, four British officers informed Elizabeth that they would be staying in her house. She and her children could make beds for themselves on the floor. She must also prepare meals for them. The rocker seemed to be the favorite place to sit among the British officers. One night when it was bitterly cold, there was no more wood to put in the fireplace. The officers looked around for something to use for firewood. One of the officers eyed the rocker. Elizabeth immediately spoke up, saying, 'That rocker is made of a native wood that is very slow to burn. I'm afraid we would freeze to death before it made a good fire.' The rocker was spared by Elizabeth's quick thinking. Sometime later, Elizabeth was in her front yard when she saw people hurrying by. They cried out in excitement that the war was over. The British had surrendered at Yorktown, and the four officers who had been staying in Elizabeth's house were gone.

"It was several weeks after that Elizabeth saw someone walking down the lane toward her house. Then with a shout of joy, she realized it was Peter. He was walking with the aid of a stout sapling and had a thick bandage wrapped around his head, but he was home. It took months for Peter to recover from his war injuries, but that day did come. From then on, Peter sat in the rocker on the front porch with Elizabeth on warm evenings to relax after a hard day's work.

"Now we go even farther back in time. My great-great-great-great-great-grandparents, Louis and Anna Nijhoff, lived in New Amsterdam. He made the rocker. Go and lift it."

I walked over to the rocker and placed both of my hands under one armrest and pulled up. I raised that one side of the rocker up just slightly.

Mrs. Wilmont smiled and said, "Look on the back of the rocker."

I did and saw the numbers 1679.

I thought for a moment then asked, "Was this rocker made in 1679?" The idea was incredible.

Mrs. Wilmont answered, "Yes, Louis made it. As you see, it is a massive piece of furniture. It was made to last, though I doubt that Louis had any idea that it would be in use this many years later. He made the rocker when Anna was expecting their first child. He also made a cradle, but somewhere along the way, it was lost. Did you notice the cushion in the seat of the rocker?"

I answered, "Yes. I looked at it and wondered if it had goose feathers in it."

Mrs. Wilmont said, "I don't know about that, but when my great-grandfather gave the rocker to my father, he told him that the covering on the cushion should be replaced as it was about one hundred years old at that time. Well, my father somehow never got around to replacing the cover, so when he gave the rocker to me, I was advised to replace the cushion. As you can see, I have done nothing about it either. It looks like it was a pretty print design at one time, but it is so faded now. I'm not sure what it looked like when it was new."

I asked Mrs. Wilmont if she ever sat in the rocker, and she replied," Oh yes, I sit in it often, but I always remove the cushion first and put another one in its place. Here, let me do that now and you sit on it."

She changed cushions, and I sat down very carefully.

She laughed and said, "I don't think your one hundred pounds is going to break that rocker. In fact, I think a three-hundred-pound person could sit in it without the least bit of stress to the rocker."

I relaxed, leaned back, and began rocking. It was comfortable, and we both laughed when my rocking to and fro brought out a squeak.

Mrs. Wilmont said, "I have always heard that a rocker is not worth a nickel if it does not squeak. I guess the squeak is what lulls babies to sleep. That is the story in short form. I decided to spare you every detail because you would be here for a much longer time.

"Sometimes when I am sitting in the rocker, I think of the trails it traveled in covered wagons, escaping Indian attacks, wars, crossing raging rivers, and rugged mountains, how many babies has it rocked to sleep, and the many wives and mothers that have rocked while thinking through some worry or problem. Now you see why it has an honored place in the house. To say that it is an attractive piece of furniture would not be the case, but it is beautiful to me. I have shared its history with our son, so when it is time for me to hand it down, he will be honored to have it in his home."

I gathered my things together and prepared to leave. "Mrs. Wilmont, this has been a most delightful afternoon. After all, it is not every day that I get to see something made in 1679. I never dreamed that I was going to have such an interesting history lesson. Thank you for sharing with me about your rocker. You know? Every time I sit in one of my rockers at home, I will think about yours and the history behind it."

Susan and Fancy

Susan had wanted a horse from the time she was a little girl. Lee and I got her a stick horse, which she rode all the time. As she grew older, the desire only increased.

Finally when we felt that she was old enough to have one, we told her that our search was on, that she was going to actually have her very own horse. Lee built a stall and a manger. Then we asked around about a horse. After some time, a friend told us of a man who had an older, gentle horse, and he was interested in selling it. We contacted the gentleman and asked some questions about the horse. He assured us that the horse was gentle, and he said that he felt that the horse would be just right for Susan, so we made a deal.

From the moment the horse arrived at our place, horse and new owner bonded. Susan spent a lot of time with Fancy, and they covered many a mile together. Lee and I laid down specific rules about riding and care of Fancy. We wanted Susan to enjoy having a horse, but we also wanted her to be safe. Time passed and the bond between those two grew deeper. Gradually we extended the distance that they could go.

One day, Susan rode Fancy to visit an elderly lady who was a friend of our family for many years. Arriving there, Susan saw that the lady was not at home. As will happen, Fancy had the urge to go to the bathroom and chose to use the lady's well-tended flower garden. Susan was determined to not leave that "deposit" there, so she went next door and asked the lady if she would be interested in some fresh fertilizer. The lady paused a moment and asked Susan to repeat what she had just said. Susan did so.

As the lady began laughing and looking at Fancy, she remarked, "I think that would be okay."

With a sigh of relief, she asked the lady if she had a shovel that she would permit Susan to use. The lady told Susan where to look, and quickly, Susan got the shovel, cleaned up Fancy's deposit, cleaned the shovel, and returned it to its proper place. Thanking the lady for taking the fertilizer and the use of her shovel, Susan mounted Fancy and went on her way before Fancy had another urge to go to the bathroom.

Susan and Fancy had many rides which were most enjoyable. A longtime dream had been fulfilled.

A Phone Call

There it was. The most attractive rolltop desk I had ever seen. It had been in the display window of a local furniture store for several weeks now. On two separate occasions, I had gone into the store just to admire it. The desk was not the kind found in an office. Rather, it was small with four spindly but decorative legs. When the top was rolled back out of the way, there were small compartments along the back of the desk, and there was just enough space on the desk to write letters or pay bills. It was not big enough to accommodate a typewriter, nor was it practical as a work desk, but still my eyes were drawn to the display window when I drove by, and I continued to wish for it.

I had mentioned to Lee several times that I sure did like that desk. One day when Lee was in town, he stopped by the furniture store and looked at the desk.

When he arrived home, he remarked, "It is not big enough to be useful."

From time to time, we had this discussion about the rolltop desk, and every time, his answer was the same. Months passed and then years went by and still, occasionally, I brought up the subject of the rolltop desk. Then something happened.

Lee had recently bought a squirrel dog named Freddie. She was eight years old, terribly bowlegged, and worst of all, Lee paid 140 dollars for her. Freddie looked like she had hunted her last squirrel some time ago. I figured that she would expire any day. However, the thought foremost in my mind was the fact that Lee had paid forty dollars more for that dog than what the rolltop desk would cost. Freddie was a sweet-natured dog, but I could not help it. Every time I looked at her, I saw this miniature rolltop desk.

One day, Lee announced that he was going to take Freddie hunting. Our youngest daughter, Susan, who was sixteen at the time, asked if she could go with him. He told her yes, and soon I watched from the kitchen window as they got in the truck and drove down our driveway. After Lee and Susan left, I went out to the clothesline and gathered all of the clothes I had hung out earlier that day. I got all of the clean clothes put away and decided to bake a pie for supper. Later as I was taking the pie out of the oven to cool, the telephone rang. It was Lee.

He said, "I happened up on a man wanting to sell his hunting dog."

I clutched the telephone tight as I asked, "What did you do?"

I could hear coins jingling in the background as Lee replied, "I bought her. Now she's not much to look at, and she is older than Freddie. In fact, I paid double what I paid for Freddie, but the man assured me that she is a real good hunting dog. I am going to stop in town and get some more dog food. After that, I will only have one dollar and twenty-eight cents in my pocket. Do you need me to pick up a gallon of milk or a loaf of bread? That's all I have money for."

As I pondered him having two old expensive hunting dogs, I envisioned that rolltop desk in our living room. Supper could just be late today. I was angry. To think that he spent a small fortune on two dogs that were likely to drop dead from old age at any time… Well, that's okay. Before this day was over, I will be admiring my new rolltop desk. I just might sit down at my new desk later this evening and answer several letters. As I was thinking of the best place to put the desk, I realized that I was still holding the telephone in my hand.

I heard Lee saying, "Mama, Mama, hello? Are you there?"

I thought fast about the best way to answer him. I tried to keep my voice normal as I spoke, "No, we don't need any milk or bread. I got both of them yesterday. However, I am on my way to town. I am going to buy me a brand-new rolltop desk." Then I hung up the telephone.

I rushed to change my clothes, put on some lipstick, and be on my way to town. I was furious. I could not get ready fast enough. I just yanked something out of the clothes closet and began changing my clothes. I was going to make one fast trip to town.

When Lee realized that I had hung up, he flew out of the telephone booth and ran to the truck where Susan was waiting. She saw the expression on his face and immediately asked what was wrong. Lee spoke not a word. He started the engine, put the truck in gear, and made swirls of dust as the truck sped onto the highway.

After a moment, he said in a very grim voice, "Watch out for your mother."

Susan knew that this was not the time to be asking questions, so she sat there wondering what in the world was the matter. After few moments, she glanced over at her father. He was sitting rigid, leaning forward toward the steering wheel. His hands were gripping the steering wheel so tightly that his knuckles were white. His eyes were glued to the road. They continued to ride on in total silence.

As they drove into town and approached the furniture store, Lee slowed the truck down and said, "Now watch closely for your mother. See if the car is parked anywhere around the store."

Finally Susan asked, "Why am I looking for Mother?"

As they slowly drove on through town, Lee answered her, "So much for your idea of a funny trick, young lady. I never had the chance to tell your mother that I was teasing, that I did not buy another dog. She is on her way now to buy that rolltop desk. I've got to stop her."

Having been convinced that I was not at the furniture store, Lee breathed a sigh of relief. Then he had a sickening thought, What if I had purchased the desk and already left? He increased the speed of the truck and rushed on toward home all the while watching every vehicle they met on the road.

I saw the truck as it came up our driveway.

Oh, piddle, I thought.

I wanted to be gone by the time they arrived. Well, I would just go out to the truck and see this wonder dog. Lee stopped the truck, and he and Susan got out. I walked outside and looked in the back of the truck. Nothing there. Did he put the dog in the cab of the truck? I did not see anything there either.

Just as I was about to ask where the dog was, Lee spoke up, saying, "Have you already been to town?"

I replied, "No, I am ready to leave now. Where is the dog?"

Lee's face showed considerable relief as he realized that there was no rolltop desk in the house.

He said, "Now, Mama, there is no dog. I did not buy one. Susan and I thought it would be funny if I called and said that I had purchased the dog. I was just teasing."

I stood there for a moment realizing that my chance for the rolltop desk was gone. If only I had left the house just a few minutes earlier.

Susan walked over to where I was standing and said, "Mom, Daddy was sure that you would arrive at the furniture store before he could get to you. I told him that I bet we would get home before you left. You always have to change clothes and put your lipstick on before you go anywhere. I have never seen you go anywhere without putting on lipstick."

I slowly went back in the house. I did not know how to feel; a part of me was relieved to know that Lee had not paid a small fortune for another dog, but another part of me almost wished he had. If I had only gone to town dressed the way I was, I would have that rolltop desk now.

Some years later, Lee offered to buy the desk. I knew that we didn't really have a place to put it, and while it was lovely to look at, it was not intended to serve the purpose as a regular desk, so I declined the offer with my thanks. Maybe sometimes, there is more pleasure in dreaming of something than really possessing it.

My Five Tomato Plants

The summer of 1980 was extremely hot and dry. By early June, we had plowed up the parched plants in our vegetable garden. A lot of people experienced the same problems that we had. Ponds dried up and livestock died. Our grass was the color of straw and sounded like cornflakes when we walked on it. Even many large trees did not survive the heat and dry weather. For over twenty days, the temperature reached over one hundred degrees by ten o'clock in the morning, continuing to rise during the day. The nights were not much better. When we went to bed, the sheets felt like they had just been taken out of a hot dryer. Everyone watched the sky, hoping for rain. Dark storm clouds would appear in the distance and thunder was heard, but no rain came.

I thought it would be nice to have a few tomato plants. That would not be too much to water, so I made a trip to a feedstore in town. I explained to a worker there what I wanted. He recommended patio tomato plants because they could be grown in the shade and were of a hearty variety. Along with the tomato plants, I purchased a large bag of potting soil and returned home.

The intense heat made me wonder if this tomato project was a good idea after all. Even if I put the plants in the shade, the hot air might be too much for them. However, since I had made the purchase, I might as well put them in pots and see what would happen.

The first thing I did was to make myself a large glass of iced tea. Then I went outside to our storage room and searched for five clay pots and trays to go with them. Sometime later, with an empty iced tea glass in hand, I stood on the carport and admired the attractive row of tomato plants. They looked very promising, and my mouth almost started watering in anticipation of the delicious tomatoes we would enjoy. However, I was glad the task was completed as the temperature was getting very uncomfortable. I reminded myself to come back out very early tomorrow morning to check on the tomatoes before the heat became unbearable.

The next morning, after Lee and I had eaten our breakfast, I walked outside with him as he left for work. It was just a little before six o'clock. I looked at the plants. There were four plants, just as I had left them the day before. The fifth plant, however, was laying across the top of the clay pot. Puzzled, I walked over and picked it up. It was not damaged in any way. I got down on my knees and made a hole in the potting soil. Carefully, I held the plant in place with one hand and packed the dirt around it with my other hand. I gave the dirt a couple of firm pats to complete the job. Suddenly I jumped. Something was not right. It was early morning, and that part of the carport was in the shade, but I thought I saw the dirt move. I pressed down again on the dirt. This time, I was sure. That dirt moved. A moment later, a frog popped out of the dirt and landed on the rim of the pot. I did not move. The frog looked around then hopped down on the carport floor. He continued on his way across our yard and under the fence. Very soon, he disappeared into the woods near our house.

I thought, *That takes care of the frog. He will not be back.*

I turned back to the tomato plant and repotted it. I went in the house and decided that it might be a good idea to go out a few times during the day and check on that tomato plant. As hot as it was, the roots would dry out quickly. Each time I looked at the plant, it was upright in the pot.

The next morning as Lee left for work, I went outside with him to see about the plants. We both stopped short. That fifth tomato plant was laying across the rim of the pot again. This time, when I patted the dirt, I did not jump when the frog popped out of the dirt. He did the same thing he had done the day before, and soon, he disappeared into the woods.

I thought, *Surely, since he had been disturbed two days in a row, he would find another place.*

I repotted the tomato plant, watered all of them, and went inside the house. The heat was even worse that day. I decided that the tomato plant was on its own. I was staying in the house and having a glass of iced tea.

Again, the next morning, very early, I went to check on the tomatoes. Four of the plants looked fine. That poor fifth plant was across the rim of the pot. That frog was very persistent. He had come to the same pot every time. I decided that I was going to have to come up with another plan instead of repotting every time.

I went into the store room and dug around for another container and tray. After I filled it with potting soil, I went to the carport. I picked up the plant from the rim of the pot and planted it in the container I had just filled with potting soil. Then I put it in the row with the other pots. Now I had four tomato plants, one pot of dirt, and last in the row was the fifth tomato plant in the newly filled pot. I just hoped this plan would work. To my relief, none of the plants were disturbed all that day. I was beginning to think that the fifth plant was going to be left alone at last.

The following day, I smiled as I stepped out on the carport. There were five tomato plants all in an upright position. Not one had been bothered. The fifth plant was smaller than the others and looked a little droopy, but I hoped that in a day or two, it would recover.

I had to water the plants nearly every day because the heat dried them out so quickly. I always watered the "frog" pot when I watered the tomato plants. Once a week, I added tomato plant food to the water, but I never used that when I watered the frog pot. For that one, I just used plain water.

Several days passed. The plants remained undisturbed. I began to wonder if the frog was even using the clay pot anymore. I had not seen anything of him for a few days. I decided that I would try to find out if he was in the pot or not. Carefully, I picked up the fifth pot. I raised it above my head. Sure enough, there was the frog. His tummy was pressed against the drain hole of the clay pot. I slowly sat the pot back down in the tray. Throughout that day, I thought about that frog and determined that I would watch him more closely. I had become interested in him.

The next morning, he arrived on time, a little before six o'clock. I stood very still and watched as he used his hind legs to make a hole in the dirt. He kept digging until he worked his way to the bottom of the pot. There he stayed where it was cool, damp, and dark all through the hot, scorching day. I think he was one happy frog. As the day changed to dusky dark, the frog popped out of the dirt, hopped on the rim of the pot, and sat there for just a moment. Then he made his way into the woods, where I suppose that he remained through-out the night.

The next day, he repeated the same pattern. In fact, that frog followed the same routine every day throughout that hot, dry sum-mer. He never varied his timing more than few minutes, morning or evening. You could almost set your watch by that frog. He never went to another pot, always the fifth one. I watched the comings and goings of that frog faithfully during the weeks of summer. I contin-ued to put water in the tray of the fifth pot every time I watered the tomato plants.

We enjoyed fresh tomatoes from those plants, except the fifth plant. It grew into a lovely full bush, loaded with green leaves, but it never produced one tomato. I guess it had gone through too much as a young plant.

The frog continued to be our "guest" until frost. At times during the winter months, I smiled when I thought about the frog and won-dered if he would return the next summer.

The summer of 1981 was as wet, and the previous year had been dry. I put a clay pot, filled potting soil on the carport just in case, but no frog came. There was no need for a frog to search for a cool, damp, dark place to rest during the day. The creeks had water in them, and the ground was often refreshed by rain. But for one summer, there was a frog that gave me considerable amusement and pleasure.

Old Cough 'N Sputter

Bad, bad news...

Lee has decided to take matters into his own hands and work on our lane. Old Cough 'N Sputter (our antiquated tractor) never cranks up on its own—oh, no. First Lee connected a chain to the front of the tractor then hooked the other end of the chain to the hitch on the back of the truck. He hurriedly waved to me to get in the driver's seat of the truck as he jumps on the tractor seat. I gently pushed on the gas pedal; the chain went taut, and we went jerking down the rough lane, hoping to hear Old Cough and Sputter's engine start up. Lee motioned for me to speed it up, or we will be all day just getting the tractor to start.

I sped up a little, and suddenly, I see Lee frantically waving his arms in a wide arch, which meant I should have stopped sooner as the tractor had started. Lee disconnected the chain, tossed it in the truck bed, and motioned toward the house. I got the truck turned around and, with a sigh of relief, headed home.

My relief at being away from the scene of action was short-lived.

Lee opened the kitchen door and said, "Mama, guess you better get the truck and help me get the tractor out of the mud. She's stuck fast."

Gritting my teeth, we got in the truck, and I drove Lee to the tractor. Oh, no, how could that much of the tractor get buried in the mud? I hoped the truck was powerful enough to do the job. Lee connected the chain then gave me instructions equal to the D-Day invasion! It is some trick to keep the truck from getting stuck in all that muck and mire while attempting to pull Old Cough and Sputter to firmer ground. Lee gave numerous changes of strategy accompanied by additional instructions, none of which I seemed to carry out very well.

Suddenly the tractor is free of mud. Truck and tractor took us flying down the hill. Lee was standing on the tractor, both hands tightly gripping the steering wheel, eyes wide with terror. He struggled to stay on the tractor, slipping and sliding with every bump, and every place his puts his feet is covered with slick, oozy mud. I was trying to keep the truck away from the ditches.

Finally I ease the truck to a stop only to see Lee still with both feet on the tractor brake pedal, making every attempt to get Old Cough and Sputter stopped before it goes into the truck bed. The tractor stopped only inches from the truck. Lee slumped down onto the tractor seat, looking like he has just finished a five hundred–yard run. Thinking it was not necessary for conversation at this point, I quickly unhooked the chain, tossed it in the back of the truck, and beat it for the house.

The Snowbirds

The icy, cold wind had been blowing hard all day. The temperature had dropped into the teens, and the sky looked dark and heavy. The weather forecast said we would probably get a light snow that evening. I made a quick trip into town to stock up on groceries, batteries, dog food, birdseed, and library books. As I left the library, I saw small snowflakes beginning to fall. I was glad that I had completed all of my errands and could start for home.

I had to drive at a slow pace because the traffic was heavier than usual, and the snow was really coming down now. It looked like someone had slit a huge feather pillow as the large flakes fell to the ground. I felt like I was in a cotton ball. If I had not been concentrating on my driving, I would have admired the different lacy patterns that the snowflakes made as they froze to the windshield.

I was quite relieved when I drove the car onto our carport. As I was unloading the car, I noticed that the snow was coming down thick and fast. It would feel good to get in the house and have a cup of hot tea.

Later Lee came in from work and remarked that the snow was still coming down, and it was getting deep. We looked outside several times during the evening. Everything in the glow of our yard light was white. We went to bed wondering if it would snow all through the night.

The next morning, we awoke to a beautiful silent world. No vehicles moved on the road. There was no sound of any outside activity. The only moving things were the many large snowflakes that were coming down. The snow was quite deep now.

Lee left for work, but he had to walk. The snow just balled up under the truck, making it immobile. Fortunately a friend saw him walking along the side of the highway and gave him a ride.

The snow continued on and on. Everything was weighted down with the wet snow. I noticed that the bird feeders were all empty. I bundled up and went outside. As I gathered up the bird feeders, I saw that even though I was wearing my old galoshes, the sixteen-inch snow came up over the tops of those boots. I quickly took the feeders into our storage room where I kept the birdfeed. After filling them, I returned each one to the places where I had them hanging.

It felt good to get back in the house. I knew that the birds would be anxious to eat. I stood and looked out of one of our den windows. Immediately five juncos, a pretty snowbird, appeared on the ground under one feeder where I had spilled some seeds while getting the feeder hung up, and those birds were quickly eating the seeds up. They were hopping around, and I laughed just watching them. Suddenly there were only four birds there. I knew that I had counted five, and I had not seen one fly away. Besides, why would one leave when there was a feast to enjoy right there? I counted again. There were only four birds. While I was trying to figure out what happened to that fifth bird, it appeared, just as quickly as it had disappeared. It looked to the left and then to the right. Then it flew up to a tree limb and sat there. I realized at that moment what had happened. As the bird was frolicking around on the ground, paying no attention to what he was doing, he had fallen into one of my sixteen-inch footsteps. When he flew out and landed on the ground, he behaved much like a human might do under the same circumstances—he looked to see if anyone had seen him make that foolish mistake.

The Squirrel

For many years, my husband Lee and I enjoyed watching the squirrels scamper around in our backyard and in the woods near our house. They would do amazing balancing acts, going at a rate of fast speed across the top of our wooden fence. I have a picture of one hanging by his toes from the roof edge of our house, stretching to reach a bird feeder. I have seen them jump from a tall bush to a bird feeder, where they stayed until they had eaten their fill. I found one on our front porch in a flowerpot, which was directly below a bird feeder. The squirrels gave as much pleasure and entertainment as the birds. Unfortunately nearly all of the squirrels have been killed off, so we seldom see one anymore. I miss them.

During the years that we did have squirrels, they were not particular about which feeder they ate from. If I failed to keep the squirrel feeders supplied with sunflower seeds, they did their very best to get to one of the many bird feeders we had hanging near the house. The squirrels were very persistent. I never failed to see one get to a bird feeder one way or the other.

One day, I hung a new bird feeder on the limb of a tree a short distance from the house. I used a narrow plastic belt as the hanger. The feeder was too far from the trunk of the tree for a squirrel to reach it. It also hung down too far from the limb for the squirrel to stretch down to it. I felt sure that I had come up with a squirrel-proof arrangement. For several days, squirrels tried their best to get to that feeder. Then one day, a new squirrel came on the scene.

I saw this small squirrel scamper across the yard, darting this way and that, sniffing as he went. He was rather comical looking because of his tail. It had almost no hair on it. He came to the tree where the new feeder was hanging. Quickly he went up the trunk and shot out

114

on the limb the plastic belt was looped over. He held onto that limb with his hind feet and reached down toward the feeder. He stretched and stretched. I could almost hear him grunting. He just could not quite reach it. He would shift his position and try again. Minutes passed and he was still trying to get to that feeder.

Then he straightened up and scurried across the limb to the trunk. He hurried down the trunk onto the ground. He stood there, looking up at the bird feeder. He made me think of a carpenter, measuring with his eyes, instead of using a tape measure as a carpenter sometimes would do. After a moment, he rushed back up the tree and out on the limb where the feeder was. Again, he held on to the limb with his hind feet while stretching just as far as he could to reach. It was no use. That feeder was out of his reach. He tried again and again with no success. Finally he came down from the tree and scampered off. I watched him disappear, wondering if he would be back.

The next day, the same squirrel appeared. At least, I think it was the same squirrel because his tail looked just like the tail of the squirrel that had come the day before. He tried every way he knew of to reach the feeder from the tree limb. Then he would scamper down to the ground and look up at the feeder. He would go back up the tree and out on that same limb, again, trying to get to it. I am sure he grew a little bit in length because he stretched so much. However, it did him no good. The feeder remained just out of his reach. Each day after he had spent considerable time attempting to get to the feeder, he would leave. I expect he felt quite put out. This went on for several days, then something happened.

I had been keeping a close watch on that squirrel. He was quite entertaining. One day, he arrived at the tree and went up on the limb as usual. I stood by the window and watched as he tried again to reach the feeder. He had no luck. Up and down the tree he went, out on the limb to stretch toward the feeder, then down to the ground to look back up at the feeder. Over and over, he persistently attempted to get to the sunflower seeds in the feeder. Then it happened.

I was casually watching that squirrel do as he had done many times before when all of a sudden, as I remained by the window, he attempted something new to reach the bird feeder. I laughed so hard that my checks felt tight. I did not even want to blink my eyes for fear I might miss something. I was watching the wonder of wildlife at its best.

That scrawny-tailed squirrel had determined that he would have some sunflower seeds from that feeder. I watched as he sat down on the limb the feeder was attached to. As he sat there, he drew that plastic belt with the feeder attached, paw over paw, just like one would draw a bucket of water out of a well. He continued to draw that bird feeder closer and closer to him. At last, he took hold of the feeder with one paw and hugged it close to his body. With his other paw, he began eating the sunflower seeds. He ate and ate. I was not positive, but it sure looked to me as though that squirrel was grinning. I stood there watching for quite a while and noticed that the squirrel never even slowed down. His paw moved quickly from the feeder to his mouth. He intended to enjoy every bite since it had taken him several days to accomplish his goal.

I continued watching the squirrel. This was royal entertainment. When the sunflower seeds were reduced to a much lower level in the feeder than before the squirrel got his hands on it. I saw him let go of the feeder. It swung back and forth along with the plastic belt it was attached to. I had to chuckle as I watched the squirrel come down from the tree. He came down very slowly. When he got to the ground, his tummy was bulging as he waddled out of sight. He was moving at a much slower pace than when he came to the tree.

I imagine that when he arrived home, his mother asked him what in the world had he been eating, and why did he eat so much? I expect she sent him to bed without supper because he had no room for another bite anyhow.

I did not expect to see that squirrel for the next several days. I figured it would take him that long to recover from the stomachache he must surely have.

The next day, however, he was back, bouncy as ever, and ready to eat again. Now everything was different. He knew the secret of how to get to those sunflower seeds. He got right to the business of drawing up the feeder to himself as he sat on the tree limb. I observed that even though he ate for quite a while, he did not eat as long as he had done the day before.

It was interesting to know that it was the same squirrel that came each day to the feeder. No other squirrel around our house had a tail like that one, and he provided many hours of delightful entertainment throughout that summer.

The Sunday I Nearly Disrupted Church

Church centennials are interesting. The First Baptist Church in Mena celebrated their centennial in 1997. A big Sunday afternoon service was planned with various committees at work covering a wide range of responsibilities. Invitations had been sent out to former pastors and their families. Former church members living out of town or out of state were informed of the service. A part of the afternoon program consisted of speakers from the Arkansas Baptist State Office. Members of the church were to dress in styles, like those that had been worn to church at any time during that one hundred–year period. A history table was set up where old church pictures and other things of interest were displayed. It was a fun and exciting time. As church organist, I searched for music that was appropriate for the occasion and perhaps would stir some memories of hymns that had not been heard for a long time. I had gone through a lot of music and had found what I wanted. Then it looked like my plans might be changed.

A specialist I had been seeing told me that I needed some minor outpatient surgery. I told him of the special church event and asked if I could wait until some later time. He advised against that. I then asked him if I would be able to get up on the organ bench and play for the centennial service. He assured me that if no complications arose, I could play, cautioning me to be very careful when I got on and off of the organ bench. I agreed to go ahead with the surgery.

I had worked hard to get the music ready in plenty of time as I felt sure I would not feel like doing any practicing for a day or so after the surgery. That only left a couple of days until Sunday. For those few days, I questioned whether I was going to feel like wearing anything except the comfortable clothes I had been wearing around the house. However, by late Saturday evening, I felt much better. I looked over my music to be sure that everything was in order.

Sunday morning, Lee and I arrived at the church. When it came time for the worship service to begin, I eased myself onto the organ bench. There were a large number of guests there, who would stay for the dinner immediately after church then attend the centennial service that afternoon. The worship service started out fine, but I did get tired and experienced some minor discomfort, but I knew that I would be able to relax during the sermon. When the pastor came to the close of his message, he did as he did at the end of all his sermons—he said a prayer before the invitation hymn was sung. This was my cue to go from the first pew, where I sat during the sermon, up to the organ. By the time he said amen, I would be on the organ bench and ready to play the introduction to the invitation hymn.

On this particular Sunday morning, as the pastor said the prayer, I quietly walked up on the platform and started to carefully ease myself onto the organ bench. I had placed my hand above the upper keyboard to brace myself while getting on the bench. Somehow, my hand slipped. I knew it would make a loud noise if my hand hit the keys. Quickly I used my foot to stop myself from falling on the organ keyboards. I aimed my foot just above the wooden pedal board, but my foot fell a little short, landing on the low *C* foot pedal.

Suddenly in the extreme quiet of the moment came this deep cannon-like sound which filled the entire church auditorium. In a split second, I removed my hand, repositioned it, and got my foot off of that pedal.

To my great relief, the pastor had continued with his prayer. It was beyond me how he could concentrate, but I had enough to worry about at the moment just trying to maintain my balance. I had just lightly placed my hands in position when I heard the amen. I played the introduction, and the music director led the choir and congregation in the invitation hymn. I tried to look as though nothing had taken place, but there was little I could do about my very red face. I could not help but notice that it sounded to me as though very few people in the congregation were singing. I glanced at the choir. The ones that were singing looked like they had on very tight collars.

Then I noticed that the pianist had stopped playing. I wondered what was going on. At last, the service ended with a benediction.

As I began playing the postlude, the music director walked over to the organ and asked me a question, "Linda, what did you do to the invitation hymn?"

I replied, "I didn't do anything."

I explained to him about losing my balance while trying to get on the organ bench. I showed him what I had done to keep from landing on the organ keys.

He looked at me, chuckled, and said, "I bet that when you shifted positions with your hand, it hit the transposer button and lowered the pitch down. The invitation hymn was so low that I could hardly sing the notes."

Just about that time, the pianist walked up to the organ, and she also asked me what had happened. She said, "I just stopped playing because the piano and the organ were not in the same key."

I felt good about one thing. If they had not seen me nearly fall all over the organ keys, hopefully, no one in the congregation had noticed me either. By this time, the pastor had greeted everyone as they left the auditorium and walked up to the organ. I apologized to him for making the disturbance during the prayer.

He laughed and said, "Was that you? I thought something had gone wrong with one of the air-conditioning units. Don't worry about the loud boom noise. I learned a long time ago to just keep going no matter what noises are made during a prayer."

I closed the organ, and in a few minutes, we made our way outside where we joined the rest of the congregation to enjoy a delicious meal while visiting with different guests. After everyone had eaten their fill, we returned to the auditorium for the centennial service. Thank goodness, I maintained my balance during that program. Everything went as planned, and a good time was enjoyed by all. By the time the centennial program came to an end, however, I was worn out and ready to go home and rest.

A week later, when I returned to the specialist for my check-up, he asked about the centennial service. I told him that the centennial service went well. Then he asked if I experienced any problems getting on and off of the organ bench. I mentioned about the morning service and how close I came to falling on the organ keys, and what a terrible noise that low *C* foot pedal made. He got his chuckle for the day over that one.

After the examination, he gave me a good report.

The next Wednesday at choir practice, I took a good deal of teasing. The following Sunday morning when it was time for the service to begin, several wary eyes watched me get on the organ bench. At the close of the service, no one was more relieved than me that there had been no mishap at the organ.

Pellor and the Storm

The dark night was peaceful and still. Pellor slowly stretched, so she would not awaken her one-week-old puppies lying nearby. Goodness knows, it was seldom that all six of them were asleep at the same time, and Pellor wanted to savor a quiet moment. She looked at them; all six were black with tan markings, almost identical. Asleep, they were a tangled mass of heads, tails, and paws. With mother close and stomachs full, their small world was just about perfect.

Suddenly Pellor raised her head and sniffed. Something was in the air. She sniffed again. A storm was coming. Pellor sensed that it was going to be a bad storm, and it was not very far away. The puppies would no longer be safe where they were. Pellor had chosen this spot in the first place because it was higher than the ground around it, but it still would not be high enough for the storm that was coming. She must decide where to move them and do it quickly because time was not in her favor, and she would have to make six trips back and forth.

Pellor considered several places, but the one she liked best was the Gandy's old storage shed. It was roomy and dry, and neither Mr. or Mrs. Gandy went in there very often. Best of all, there was an opening near the back of the shed where one sheet of tin had come loose at the bottom. It had been twisted back making an opening, where Pellor could easily come and go unseen.

To get the puppies to the shed, Pellor must cross a shallow creek bed, and that could be a problem when heavy rains came. During a storm, it quickly became a deep rolling stream. Would Pellor have enough time to cross it six times, carrying each puppy by the nape of its neck?

Her mind made up. Pellor quietly picked up a puppy with her teeth, causing the other five puppies to wake up. Easing the puppy back down to the ground, Pellor explained to them that she must get them to higher ground because of the approaching storm. She would be back as quickly as possible, but they were to *stay right there and be quiet*. With that motherly admonition, Pellor again picked up the puppy and disappeared into the night.

Except for dodging brier patches and low branches, the trip to the shed was easy. The wind was beginning to stir, and Pellor heard faint rumblings of thunder in the distance. Pellor quickened her pace, and soon, she was easing through the opening of the shed. Looking all around, Pellor quickly chose a snug warm place behind some tall boxes. It could not have been a more protected spot if Pellor had prepared it herself. The boxes would hide them from view, and there would be plenty of room for the puppies. Best of all, the spot was very close to the opening near the back of the shed.

Feeling a great relief, Pellor sat the puppy down, reassured her, and left the shed to return to the other five.

Pellor could travel faster alone, and she ran through the woods. The way was more familiar to her now, and she remembered the places she needed to duck, go around, or jump over. The shallow creek bed was just another step along her way.

As Pellor came up to the place where she had left the other puppies, she saw them wiggling around and whimpering. Giving each puppy several loving licks with her tongue, she picked up another puppy and was on her way. The wind was getting stronger now, and the frequent thunder was louder. Pellor ran faster, watching closely for any sign of danger. She rushed across the shallow creek bed and pushed against the wind. Reaching the shed at top speed, she slipped inside. With the two puppies curled up next to each other, Pellor went on her way.

Another easy run through the woods, and before long, she was standing near the other four puppies. Talking to them for just a few moments, Pellor picked up the third puppy and began her trip back to the shed. By now, the wind was blowing so hard, it caused branches to sway wildly, sometimes snapping them into broken pieces. The thunder boomed like cannons, and Pellor wondered how much time she had before the storm would break in all its fury. She was getting tired, and her jaws ached from holding each puppy with the firm grip of her teeth. She eased through the opening of the shed and placed the puppy next to the others, gave a quick look around, then left.

To her dismay, Pellor felt cold rain hitting her. It was pelting down in sheets, and this was not good. She was only half done with this night's work, and the rain would slow her down. She felt relief that three of her puppies were safe and warm. Her concern for the remaining three puppies caused Pellor to take risks that would get her back to them quicker. Stepping across the shallow creek bed, Pellor saw a trickle of water making a zigzag pattern along the ground. She kept running, panting for breath and struggling to stay in the right direction.

As Pellor moved toward the remaining three puppies, a bright flash of lightning let her see that they were huddled close together and safe. She ran to them and quickly moved two of them to a place that was just a little higher. Then she nudged them under a large bush with thick branches, hoping they would be safe until she returned.

Picking up the fourth puppy, Pellor turned in the direction of the shed and started off at top speed. She was very sure of the way by now, but the severe storm made it almost impossible to make much headway. Pellor dodged one way and then another, but some of the briers and brambles made deep cuts in her skin. She ducked her head this way and that to keep the puppy free of the violently swaying branches. With one jump at full speed, Pellor left the trickling stream behind her, but she noticed that it had become wider and deeper. A mighty clap of thunder made Pellor stop short. The ground beneath her seemed to shake, and the lightning was so intense that it turned the night into day. The hair on Pellor's neck and back stood up. Slowly she crept on. There was a strong smell of smoke in the air. She looked all around, and then she saw in the distance a fire rising high in the stormy night sky. Lightning must have struck a tree, but the fire could not spread in all this hard rain. Rushing on, she came at last to the shed and gently sat the puppy down.

Pellor was soaked, panting, and tired through every inch of her body. The cuts were burning, and she longed to hide under something to get away from the lightning, but her most difficult work was still ahead of her.

The next trip would be the hardest. She would have to leave one puppy all alone while she carried the other one to the safety of the shed. If only she could carry two at a time. Would the last puppy be safe until she returned? Pellor felt sure that she would not ever feel rested or dry again.

She found the last two puppies exactly where she had left them. The branches of the large bush were serving as an umbrella and providing a safe enough place for now, but Pellor could not ease her guard or slow her pace. They were not beyond danger yet.

She looked at the two puppies and decided to leave the larger of the two for that last trip to the shed. Pellor took a few valuable moments to reassure that puppy, reminding him that she would be back just as soon as she could. He must stay there and be very quiet. Nuzzling him with her nose, she then picked up the fifth puppy. With a heavy heart, she left the last puppy there, alone and scared. The storm soon drowned out his whimpering, but Pellor could hear him in her mind all along the way. She did not let herself think of the storm and tried hard not to think of the puppy. She focused her thoughts on the stream that they had yet to cross. She heard it before she saw it. Ahead of her was an angry rolling stream. Pellor hesitated only a moment before making a fast running leap, just clearing the stream by inches. She collapsed on the other edge and took a brief pause to catch her breath. Then she made sure that the puppy was unhurt. Fear and anxiety spurred Pellor on. The last puppy must not be left to the mercy of the storm or other animals.

Reaching the shed, Pellor had hardly placed the fifth puppy with the others before she swiftly passed through the opening and sped through the cold, wet night. She tried to pace herself to conserve her little bit of remaining strength. Coming upon the stream, Pellor's heart pounded harder to see how wide it had become. She doubted that a greyhound could jump across it now. Restlessly, she paced up and down along the edge, searching for a place to get across.

A thought kept going through her mind, Was her lone puppy still safe? Had some predator found the tiny puppy alone and unprotected?

Just when she was about ready to jump in and try to swim to the other side, Pellor saw a spot where she thought she just might make it across. She yelped for joy. Moving back from the edge of the water, Pellor took a running jump. While she was midair, she looked down and saw the stream passing beneath her. Extending her front legs forward with a full stretch, Pellor braced herself for a hard landing. With a heavy thud, she hit the ground on the other side, trembling with relief but unhurt. Pellor made a mental note of the spot for her return trip with the last puppy. Then she raced on.

At last, she could see the bush a little distance away. Pellor looked all around, but no puppy was there. She sniffed the ground and looked again. She saw nothing. She heard nothing. Frantically she whimpered softly then whimpered again. Pellor thought she heard a faint whimper in reply. She barked softly and heard another whimper. She moved silently in the direction of the whimper, and there he was. What a sight to see; he was wet, muddy, and shaking all over but unhurt.

Pellor spoke softly, explaining that they must hurry as much as possible. That meant that he would have to be still as Pellor carried him along. He must not wiggle or whimper to get down. The puppy seemed to understand that this was a serious time.

Pellor took just a moment to stand and listen. She could not remember a worse storm. The lightning cracked and snapped. The thunder boomed across the entire sky. Pounding rain beat against her, and the wind was so strong that she wondered if she was going to be lifted off the ground.

As she picked up the sixth and last puppy, Pellor felt a gladness. This time, she was leaving no puppy behind. The path was cluttered with fallen branches, causing Pellor to have to slow down and watch her footing. She felt concern knowing that the stream was rising higher and higher. She wanted to get this puppy to the safety of the shed, and she was anxious about the other five. On and on, she went, making her way as fast as she could in the storm.

She heard the roar of the angry rolling stream. Pellor's heart sank. The place where she had jumped across on her last trip was now under water. Frantically she ran along the water's edge, searching eagerly for a possible place to cross. Then Pellor stopped. She blinked her eyes. The storm must have caused a large tree to fall. It spanned the stream, making a beautiful bridge for Pellor. Relief almost made her weak, but she had no time to lose. The water was lapping up over both sides of the fallen tree. Soon the tree would be completely under water. Making guttural sounds, she warned the puppy to be very still. Carefully Pellor stepped up onto the fallen tree. Step by step, she moved, trying to keep her balance. Halfway across, the night was illuminated by a blinding flash of lightning. Oh, how Pellor wished that they were already safe in the shed. Inch by inch, Pellor moved along. Then with a joyous leap, she was across.

Picking up her speed, she thought, *I'll not have to worry about that stream again this night for the shed is well beyond its reach.*

The rest of the trip was much easier. Pellor hurried along, still mindful of any sign of danger. Then there it was; that shed had never looked so good to Pellor.

She eased through the opening and moved swiftly behind the boxes. As she sat the puppy down, she made a quick count. Yes, all six were safe and sound. Pellor spoke to them, saying that she would not have to leave them again. Then a very weary Pellor dropped down next to them and was instantly asleep.

Pellor's long night's work was done and well done at that. As the storm raged outside, and the rain pounded against the tin roof, all was peaceful and still inside the Gandy's shed.

Some hours later, Pellor awoke and slowly stretched, so she would not awaken her puppies. Goodness knows, it was seldom that all six of them were asleep at the same time.

Thus begins the adventures of Pellor and her puppies.

Pellor and Her Puppies Are Found

Six roly-poly puppies came bounding around the corner of the house, responding to the signal that meant it was mealtime. Only when Mrs. Gandy whistled and clapped her hands did it mean it was time to eat. With eager faces and their tales wagging, they gathered around as their feed bowls were placed before them. While they were enjoying their food, Mrs. Gandy watched them from nearby and let her thoughts wonder back three months to the time Mr. Gandy had found the one-week-old puppies in their old storage shed.

Suddenly Mrs. Gandy's thoughts were brought back to the present with the sounds of whimpering puppies. Putting more feed in their bowls, Mrs. Gandy thought of the problem at hand.

The owner of Pellor told Mr. Gandy that Pellor was a very independent, free-spirited dog and never let a human close to her. They were not interested in keeping the puppies, so Mrs. Gandy asked if she might keep them. The owner said that she was welcomed to them. Mrs. Gandy's plan was to keep the puppies until Pellor weaned them then find good homes for them. However, it did not turn out that way.

Mrs. Gandy went to the shed several times a day to check on the puppies. Pellor had put them behind a tall stack of empty boxes. They had fresh air from the opening in the back of the shed but were completely hidden from view. They could not have been in a better place if Pellor had arranged the whole thing herself. There was just one thing that bothered Mrs. Gandy. Each time she went into the shed, Pellor was never there with the puppies. A quick search revealed Pellor hiding in some tall grass just behind the shed. When it was almost dark, Pellor would move quickly into the shed, where she remained all night. Then when the first rays of daylight shone in the sky, she left to return to the tall grass and watch the shed until it became dark again.

Well, this would never do, thought Mrs. Gandy. *One-week-old puppies should not go all day without something to eat.* She decided to help Pellor out by calling their veterinarian to ask him what to do.

The vet said that while the puppies would survive, they sure would get hungry. Mrs. Gandy asked what she could do for the puppies. After receiving the feeding information she needed, she thanked the veterinarian and made a trip to town.

A few hours later, holding a baby bottle containing puppy formula, Mrs. Gandy went to the shed to begin feeding the puppies. Then a thought occurred to her. Those puppies were identical. How could she tell which puppy she had fed and which ones had not been fed? She rushed back into the house and cut some yarn into six pieces. Once again, she went to the shed and soon had a puppy eagerly drinking the formula. When the bottle was empty, a piece of yarn was tied on one of the puppy's legs. It was not too tight; just snug enough to stay on. Washing the bottle after each puppy was fed took some extra time, but eventually, all the puppies had taken their measure of formula and were now sound asleep with full tummies. Now it would be easy to remove the pieces of yarn and save them until the next feeding.

When the puppies were two weeks old, the vet said it was time to give them worm medicine.

Mrs. Gandy stopped by his office to get the medicine and, on her way home, thought about how she was to get this task done. She decided to put up a temporary pen using decorative fencing left over from the flower garden. It was not very high but then neither were the puppies. It should do just fine. Once the pen was completed, Mrs. Gandy thought it would be a good idea to use the pieces of yarn, so she would know for sure which puppy had been given worm medicine and which ones had not had theirs yet.

Things were going smoothly. There were two puppies in the pen, and the third one was getting his medicine. Just as Mrs. Gandy turned to place the third puppy in the pen, she stopped short and looked around. There were no puppies in the pen. There was no way they could get over the fencing that made up the pen. Just where in the world were those two puppies? Holding the third puppy, Mrs. Gandy made her way to the shed. Sure enough, there they were, safe and sound. It seemed that Pellor did not like her puppies taken out of the shed and put in the pen, so she came out of the tall grass, slipped up behind Mrs. Gandy, and took one puppy at a time to the back of the shed. It was hard to say who was the busiest, Mrs. Gandy or Pellor. However, after some time, all the puppies were given their medicine.

As the puppies grew, the vet suggested that some baby cereal with milk mixed in with the softened puppy food would be good for them. They lapped it up quickly, always looking for more. They were healthy puppies.

Time passed, and suddenly one day, Mr. Gandy stated that it was time to find homes for the puppies since Pellor had weaned them. Mrs. Gandy felt a tight knot in the pit of her stomach. She realized that she had become very attached to those puppies, and she did not like the idea of giving them away. During those eight weeks, she had watched them grow and become playful with each other. She just could not part with them. Many discussions about the puppies took place over the next several weeks. Mr. Gandy said to pick one puppy to keep and give the others away. How in the world could you pick one? Which one would stay, and which ones would be taken off? There was no way to choose just one.

Time went on and so did the discussions. Mr. Gandy was holding firm that they just could not keep six puppies who would grow into six big dogs. Mrs. Gandy continued to say that she just could not part with the puppies after taking care of them for eight weeks. All the while, the puppies continued to grow and develop their own individual personalities.

At last, the time came when Mr. Gandy said that the puppies could stay and just in time too as cold weather was approaching. Mrs. Gandy moved six doghouses on the carport and noticed that each puppy had its favorite house. Hay was stored on the carport, ready for the really cold temperatures. When it came time to pile it into the doghouses, the puppies could burrow down into the hay and keep warm. Mrs. Gandy decided that when the biting winter wind blew across the carport, she would put their feed bowls inside the doghouses when it was time for them to eat.

It was fun to watch them frolic around in the yard. They came on the run when the "mealtime" signal was given. They were very mannerly when it came to their evening snacks. Each one waited for his or her name to be called before coming up to Mrs. Gandy for their treat. They had a large yard to play in with fields and woods nearby for exploring. Best of all, they were home, and that is how Pellor's puppies came to be permanent residents at the Gandys.

One Missing Puppy

One puppy was missing that morning when I went outside to feed them.

I noticed that Wet Paw was not with his other five littermates. This was unusual. They were always in the yard, and most of the time, they stayed fairly close to each other. At six months of age, they were well accustomed to my signal of clapping my hands together and whistling when it was time to eat. This brought the puppies on the run. This morning, however, I did not give the signal. I began walking around the yard, searching for Wet Paw. I immediately became aware that there were five hungry puppies going right along with every step I took. After a short search for Wet Paw, I returned to the storage room on the carport and filled their feed bowls. Then I called the puppies by name as I placed each bowl down on the carport. There was Bashful, Longface, Mr. Manners, Nipper, and Waddles. Wet Paw's filled bowl remained on the table in the storage room. While the puppies were happily eating their food, I put fresh water in their drinking tub then continued my search for Wet Paw. A thorough search of the yard, pasture, and wooded area provided no clue as to his whereabouts.

Returning to the carport, I noticed that Bashful and Waddles were lying there with their heads across their empty bowls. The other three was just sitting there, waiting. I filled their bowls again and chuckled as they began munching on their food. Later with their stomachs full, they ambled to comfortable places in the yard, curled up, and immediately went to sleep. I gathered up the bowls and took them to the storage room. After putting the lid on the feed barrel, I went into the house.

Frequently during the day, I went outside and searched for Wet Paw. Each time, I clapped my hands and whistled for several minutes, but Wet Paw was gone. By late afternoon, I was really getting uneasy. I went out to the side yard, where Lee was at work in his machine shop, and told him that I was going to drive around the neighborhood in hopes of finding Wet Paw.

In a few minutes, I was driving slowly through the neighborhood and calling out for Wet Paw. I would then pause and listen. I thought that maybe he would bark if he heard my voice. After I made two circles around the neighborhood and there was no sign of Wet Paw, I returned home. As I drove into the driveway, it was my hope that I would see him in the front yard, wagging his tail. But there was no Wet Paw. Soon it would be dark, and I really dreaded for him to be out because he was black and tan colored, and it would be hard for anyone to see him. He did have on a collar with identification on it.

Parking the car in the carport, I got out and walked around the yard with the five puppies following each step I took. There was no sign of Wet Paw, and it was pretty obvious that the other puppies were ready to eat again.

I filled their bowls, and they did not hesitate about eating. While they were doing that, I walked to the far corner of the backyard and, again, clapped my hands and whistled. I did this for several minutes but to no avail. Wet Paw was just not anywhere around, or was he! Out of the corner of my eye, I saw something move in the tall grass just beyond the fence. I moved closer to get a better look. There was Wet Paw, but what a pitiful sight he was. He was whimpering and trembling all over. His head hung low, and he could barely walk, limping badly on two legs.

I ran to him, and he tried to wag his tail a little. I quickly looked him over. I saw no bleeding nor felt any broken bones, so I ran to the storage room for his feed bowl and then got a small container and put some water in it. I hurried back to Wet Paw and offered him the water and food. He ate some food but nearly emptied the water bowl. I waited a few minutes, so he could rest then helped him to the carport. Grabbing a piece of an old comforter and some old towels, I made him a soft bed in his doghouse. It took him several moments just to get in his doghouse. He continued to whimper and tremble. He tried three times to lie down but yelped out in pain each time, so he sat down in the very back of his doghouse. I went in the house and called the vet, but it would be the next afternoon before he could see Wet Paw. How I dreaded the long wait because I knew that Wet Paw was hurting.

During the rest of the evening, I went out on the carport several times to check on Wet Paw. He finally did manage to lie down even though he kept whimpering. Sometime later at bedtime, when I went out to check on him, he was asleep and had stopped whimpering. I decided that I had better sleep on the couch in the den which adjoined the carport. Hopefully I would hear him if he got worse during the night and cried out. Several times, I awoke and decided to go out and check on him. Each time, he was asleep, and there was no whimpering. That relieved me some, but it was still a long night.

Early the next morning, I hurried out to see how Wet Paw was doing. He wagged his tail a little, and I could see that he had eaten a small amount of the food and had taken some water. I felt that this was a good sign. He seemed content to stay in his doghouse and lie still. I made several trips outside during the morning hours to see how he was doing. After Lee and I had lunch, it was time to take Wet Paw to the vet's office.

I spread a sheet across the front seat of the car, and Lee carried Wet Paw and laid him down on the sheet. Fortunately the drive to the vet's office took only a few minutes. When we arrived, I eased out of the car and went inside. I told the receptionist that I had Wet Paw outside in the car.

She asked, "Can Wet Paw walk in here?"

I replied, "No, he can't."

She said that she would have the vet come out to the car and get him. I returned to the car to wait. After a little while, the vet came to the car with a leash in hand. He asked if I thought Wet Paw could walk, and I told him that I did not think so.

He gave Wet Paw a brief go over and said, "You are right, he can't walk. I'll carry him into the examining room."

I went ahead to open the office door. Then the examination began.

After the examination, the vet said that he could find no internal injuries or broken bones but stated, "I don't know what has happened, but Wet Paw has taken a terrific wallop. It may have come from another animal, or he might have been bumped by a car, or it could have been done by a human. But every muscle is bruised and inflamed, but his legs are the worst. I can tell you this, it took everything he had to get back home. He is totally exhausted. I am going to give him a shot now and some medicine for you to give him. Then I need to see him again in a week. Do you have a place where you can keep him penned up for at least a week?"

I replied, "Yes, we have a dog pen where I can put him." Then I asked, "Do you think his injured legs will be okay?"

The vet thought for a moment and replied, "At this point, I cannot tell you for sure, but we will do everything we know to do to get Wet Paw back to his normal self."

I assured the vet that I would have Wet Paw back in a week. Then the vet carefully picked Wet Paw up and carried him back to the car. On the way home, I thought how relieved I was to know that he had no broken bones or internal injuries, but I wondered how long it would take for the bruised muscles to heal.

By that time, I was turning into our driveway, and I noticed that even though Wet Paw was lying down on the car seat, he raised his head and wagged his tail a little as we neared home. Lee came to the car, and I told him what the vet had said about Wet Paw. Then Lee carried him to another doghouse while I got the dog pen ready for him. That took me a while. The pen had not been used for quite some time. I cleared out fallen tree branches and some thorny wild plants that had come up. Then I dragged Wet Paw's doghouse to the pen. Next came his water and feed bowls along with a few of the dog toys I had bought some time ago. Now everything was ready. Lee carried him into the pen, and I supported Wet Paw as he struggled to get in his house. Immediately he got over in a corner and laid down.

Lee returned to his workshop. I stayed until Wet Paw became accustomed to the pen. Sometime later, I left the pen and returned to the house, but I went back often during the remainder of the day. Each time I checked on him or gave him medicine, he was always lying on the same spot in his house. Most of the time he was asleep. I remembered that the vet had said that one of the medications for Wet Paw would make him sleepy.

I later got the flashlight and took some ham from the refrigerator and put it in a plastic bag and started for the dog pen. As I walked across the yard in the dark, I shone the light toward the pen. There in the beam of light were five pair of eyes staring at me. It startled me for a moment, then I chuckled. The other five puppies had gone to the pen and were lying near the gate. I went into the pen, and as I neared his house, I heard Wet Paw's tail thumping against the wall of the doghouse. I bent down and looked in. Wet Paw was lying down, but he seemed to be somewhat more comfortable. I took the ham from my pocket and offered him some. His tail began wagging faster as he smelled the ham. He ate all that I offered him, and I gave him a pretty generous portion. After I visited with him for a short while and made sure he had enough food and water, I left the pen and gave the other five puppies some of the ham, which they too enjoyed. As I started back to the house, I noticed that all five puppies stayed right there by the pen. Thinking of the distance from the pen to the house, I decided that it might be a good idea for me to sleep on the couch another night. At least, I would not be as worried as I had been the night before.

I awoke several times during the night and made my way to the pen. Wet Paw was asleep. The other five puppies were also asleep right there by the gate of the pen. Once when I returned to the couch, I just could not go back to sleep. I laid there for quite a while, thinking that I was sure going to be sleepy tomorrow. The next thing I knew, sunlight was streaming in through the windows. I got up and fixed breakfast for Lee and me. Then I went straight to the pen. The five puppies had moved away from the gate, but Wet Paw was still lying down in the back of his house. He did not appear to be interested in moving at all. I filled his feed and water containers, talked to him for a little while, and gave him his medicine. Then I returned to the house to get some housework done. Several times during the day, I walked to the pen to see about Wet Paw. This was the way each day went. Each evening, just before I went to bed, I took Wet Paw and the other puppies some treats. The puppies spent four nights by Wet Paw's pen. Then they returned to their usual sleeping place and so did I. Finally the week was over. It was time to return to the vet's office, so he could check Wet Paw.

This trip was not so difficult. Wet Paw was moving about some on his own but still limped badly whenever he put his weight on the two sore legs. I drove up next to the vet's office door so Wet Paw could walk, and I let him take his time getting in. The vet was glad to see that Wet Paw had improved in the one week but advised another week in the pen because of the extensive injury to his two legs. He instructed that I was to continue with the medicine then telephone him in another week.

I drove home with Wet Paw leaning on my shoulder. As I drove into the driveway, Wet Paw looked out the window, his tail wagging. He was home. After we got out of the car, I walked Wet Paw down to the pen. He did not hesitate for a moment and appeared glad to go in. Perhaps he felt safer in the pen after what he had experienced a week earlier.

The second week went much like the first week. I visited him often throughout each day, gave him his medicine, and made sure he had plenty of food and water. He did not want to play with his toys. He slept a lot and seemed content to just be still. I continued the bedtime treats. At the end of the week, I called the vet and told him about Wet Paw. The vet asked me if Wet Paw was using his sore legs any more often. I replied that he was not; in fact, he apparently had no desire to get on those legs.

The vet said, "I hate to keep him penned up, but it looks like he needs another week in the pen. After this next week, he will have taken all the medicine I gave you, and he should not need any more. Give me a call in a week."

I wondered how Wet Paw was going to take being in the pen for another week. I had no need for concern as he made no attempt to get out when I entered or left the pen. So began the third week.

Again, the pattern was the same—medicine, food and water, visits and treats every night before I went to bed. I noticed that Wet Paw moved about just a little more but still limped badly. I was becoming very concerned that he was going to be that way for the rest of his life. At the end of the week, I made a telephone call to the vet's office.

I heard him say, "Linda, I know you are tired of this, but I think that Wet Paw needs one more week in the pen to give his legs every chance to heal. Call me in another week."

I continued the routine that I had done for three weeks. On the second day of the fourth week, I had an idea. I went to the telephone and called the vet. I asked him if I could massage Wet Paw's two injured legs and if I could put him on a leash and walk him around the yard for a brief time.

The vet replied, "If you have the time, both ideas are good. Walk him for about ten minutes, two or three times a day." Then he told me how to massage Wet Paws legs.

I did this for the rest of the week. Each day, I hoped to see a change in him when we walked, but there was very little, if any difference. At the end of the week, I made the call to the vet's office.

After some discussion, the vet said, "Linda, we have done everything possible for Wet Paw. He has healed as much as he is going to. It is time to turn him loose. He may be crippled for the rest of his life, but I have seen a number of three-legged dogs get along okay. At least, Wet Paw has all four of his legs."

After I hung up the telephone, I went outside and hurried down to the pen. I could hardly wait to let Wet Paw out. When I entered the pen, I did not close the gate behind me as I had done for four weeks. I left it open.

I walked over to Wet Paw and said, "Come on, ole boy, you are free to go. You can get out of here."

He just sat there and looked at me. I walked over to the gate and called for him to come. He took two limping steps, stopped, and sat down.

I thought, *I can't carry you out of here.*

I had imagined that he would be very eager to return to the yard and play with his littermates. I stepped out of the pen into the yard and clapped my hands while calling for him to come to me. He sat there for a moment, then got up, and limped out of the pen. I left the gate open, so I could go back later and move his house and toys to the carport and put his bowls back in the storage room. I watched Wet Paw as he slowly moved nearer the carport. The other puppies walked over to him and greeted him back to the group by licking his nose. As Wet Paw limped across the yard toward the house, getting familiar with things and bushes again, I noticed his limp was not any better. I went into the house and did some ironing.

Later that day, I went outside to check on Wet Paw. He was nowhere to be seen. I began to panic. Surely, he had not gone away again with his legs still so sore. I looked all around the yard. Then I had a thought. I ran down to the dog pen, and sure enough, there he was in his doghouse. I left him there. I decided that he would come out sooner or later and then I could bring everything back to the house. Sometime later, he did leave the pen, and I rushed down there and brought everything back to its proper place. His house was back on the carport, his bowls were in the storage room, and his toys back in the box on the carport.

After two more weeks had passed, Wet Paw was still limping. One day, I was looking out the kitchen window as I washed the dishes. Suddenly the puppies started barking, and all of them but Wet Paw ran across the front yard toward the fence. He continued to bark but just sat there as the other five puppies stepped between the boards of the fence and ran across our meadow. After a few moments, Wet Paw stood up. I stopped doing the dishes and just watched him. He moved slowly, limping as usual. He got to the fence and carefully stepped between the boards just as the others had done moments before. Then he started running, slowly at first then faster and faster. He disappeared from my view, so I ran out on the front porch. As I stood there and watched. I saw Wet Paw continue to run. He not only caught up with the others, he passed them. He was running strong and straight with no sign of a limp. What a lovely sight that was. I just stood there and took pleasure in the thought that the long month of confinement in the dog pen had at last paid off. Wet Paw was completely healed and could again run like the wind.

Today Wet Paw is over five years old, and from that day when I stood on our front porch and watched him run across the meadow, he has not limped again.

The Stray

I looked out of the kitchen window, blinked, and looked again. There was a strange dog coming up our driveway, trotting straight for the house just like he lived here. He looked healthy and well-fed, but he wore no collar where I could get a name or phone number.

I thought, *We sure don't need another dog.*

So I called around the neighborhood to see if anyone was missing a dog, or if they might be interested in having a dog. No luck on either question, except for one lady who lived on the highway. She told me that the dog had been at her house for the past week, but she didn't know where he came from; and she was afraid of dogs, so she was not interested in keeping him.

When it was feeding time for our dogs, I found an extra water bowl, cleaned it, and fed the "guest." He was very friendly, and I could quickly become attached to him. I called the local radio station and placed an ad about the dog. Several days passed and I was beginning to lose hope of finding him a good home. Then one day, I got a phone call from a lady saying that she was interested in coming to our house and seeing the dog. I gave her directions, and soon, the lady and her daughter arrived. We introduced ourselves, and at that time, the dog came around the corner of our house.

The lady, whose name was Sharon, drew in a deep breath and exclaimed, "Oh, what a nice-looking dog."

Well, the dog was already standing next to her, wagging his tail.

Sharon said, "He is just what I want. I'll take him." Turning to the dog, she said, "I brought a collar for you in the event that I would take you. Your name is now Sparky."

After she got the collar around Sparky's neck, she leaned over and gave him a hug. Sharon opened the truck door, and Sparky hopped in just as though he had been in that truck many times. Sharon thanked me, and they drove off. I could see Sparky as they left, and he looked happy.

The next night, Sharon called and thanked me again for the dog. She said that Sparky was well mannered and good-natured. She was delighted to have him. Sharon continued to call weekly and let me know how she and Sparky were enjoying each other.

I was so thankful that Sparky had a loving home. I never found out where he came from, but I was so glad to know where he ended up.

And How Can I Help You?

I think the year was 2001—but I am not certain—that a medical team from our church planned a mission trip to Romania. It was decided that they would conduct a mock clinic in the fellowship hall of our church and have church members come with imaginary illness and health problems, so the medical team could practice. I thought that was a good idea and went to the church on the appointed time.

There was a line of church members waiting to be checked over. Finally my turn came, and I was directed to a lady (it was Sue Rowe, a church member) seated behind a table.

She smiled and said, "Please tell me your name, and how can I help you?"

Without a previous thought, I replied, "My name is Eurina Umdover." And then I began naming every ailment I could think of.

By this time, the lady was covering her mouth in an attempt to refrain from bursting out laughing. Well, I just kept on naming off my supposed reasons for coming to the clinic.

Suddenly the lady stood up and said, "Please excuse me for a moment."

She went out into the hall where two men (Bro. David and Dr. Lochala) were talking. Almost immediately, I heard laughter coming from the hall. I sat there in my chair and waited for the lady to return.

After a few minutes, she came back, sat down, and said, "Mrs. Umdover, you have numerous concerns, and they need to be addressed by a physician so we will schedule a time that you can come back."

That ended my participation in the mock clinic, *but* there have been many times of laughter at the recall of that event.

Since that day, whenever Sue and I see each other, she would say, "Why, hello, Eurina, how are you today?"

I always replied, "Hello to you, Gwendelyn," which was a name she uses between the two of us ever since that day of the mock clinic.

Tornado

I had an appointment to get a perm that Thursday morning. While Cindy worked on my hair, we talked about the weather and the tornado watch for our area. The clouds looked angry, rolling and churning across the sky. A few hours later, with a new hairdo, I left Cindy's and did a few errands in town before going home.

All through the day, the warnings appeared on TV. About 5:00 p.m., I walked outside to look at the sky. There was that greenish color in the clouds indicating that a tornado was possible. We finished supper, and I washed the dishes. I checked outside to secure things that were loose and then got candles and flashlights ready.

At 7:10 p.m., we heard the first warning siren go off. The radio stated that tornadoes had been sighted near Cove and were moving toward Mena. Reports were of winds from 130–165 miles per hour. I went outside again and looked around. The sky looked angry with dark rolling clouds. The wind was increasing, and the sky was constantly lit up from the flashes of lightning. The thunder rumbled over the mountain and across the valley. During the next hour, the sirens sounded three more times. The wind became so strong here at the house that Lee said we had better get in the front bathroom. I took a quick look outside, and even though it was after 8:00 p.m., there was a whitish look with things flying through the air. I saw nothing but leaves, twigs, and dirt swirling everywhere.

We stayed in the bathroom for about four minutes and lost electricity. During that time, Jeff and Denise came to our house while we were in the bathroom. They thought their house had been hit, and they saw the funnel as they were coming to our house.

After the storm passed through, Jeff went to his shop, called the Hicks who live down the road from us, and asked them to call us and let us know that his business was destroyed except for the offices. The coffee pot was still sitting on top of the microwave, which was in one of the offices. Lee went to Jeff's shop to help. About midnight, he returned home and said we would load our generator in our truck bed, so Lee could take it to Jeff as he was going to stay the rest of the night in the offices of his shop. Our neighbor, Randy Carter, saw the truck headlights and drove over to see if he could help. He took over my part of trying to get the generator in the truck.

While they were doing that, a car drove up, and it was Mrs. Keith, another neighbor whom I had never met. The wind was much calmer, and the lightning was less. I looked out the windows and saw that one large oak tree in our side yard had been uprooted with a large amount of dirt with it. Fortunately it fell away from the house. We began calling to see if friends and folks around us were okay. Jesse Reid came by about 10:15 p.m. to see if we were okay. The radio was already giving reports of major damage on Reine Street, DeQueen Street, and Main Street. The old Garmon house on Reine Street was flattened, killing one man. Zeke, Otha Lee Cummings, and son Bill lived in that house for many years. The Skyline Cafe sign, which has hung at the café since 1923, is still there, rusty from age but intact. Pappaw's store, Mack's Grocery, had storefront damage. I could not tell about possible roof or interior damage. Our church (First Baptist Church) was damaged, but we were able to have Sunday morning service in the fellowship hall. The Arkansas Disaster Team, Red Cross, Salvation Army, and Arkansas Baptist Disaster Relief Teams worked from our church. Tyson brought an 18-wheeler and parked in the parking lot, distributing boxes of chicken to people whose houses were destroyed or damaged. Volunteers from Virginia, Montana, and other states came to help. Baptist Church groups came from different parts of the state to assist.

The efforts of people coming to help from other areas was amazing. The First Methodist Church and the Presbyterian Church were damaged. Janssen Park took another hit, uprooting most all of the trees that escaped the 1993 tornado. The cabin was damaged again, but the clock is okay.

The courthouse, city hall (the old post office), Mena Middle School (the old high school), Janssen Park, Wal-Mart, Attwoods, RMCC, the hospital, US Motors, and Gilchrist Tractor were either destroyed or badly damaged. Over six hundred homes were destroyed or severely damaged. There were three deaths and thirty injuries. On Friday, no KCS trains ran through Mena.

Police and National Guard patrolled the railroad crossings, barring anyone from going across the tracks until Friday evening when debris was cleared enough for emergency crews and disaster relief teams to get in the area and make a door-to-door check and clear trees out of the streets so repair efforts could begin.

Friday, James Camathan came by to check on us. There was a text message on my cell phone from our granddaughter Laura. She had awakened at about 2:00 a.m. and could not go to sleep, wondering if we were okay. At that time, neither the landlines nor cell phones were workable as the towers were down, so she could not reach us. The Acorn Water Department came by to see if we needed anything, offering bottles of water. I told them we were okay but expressed my thanks for what they were doing.

Reports continued to come over the radio of damaged areas. Our electricity was restored at ten fifteen, Saturday morning. We had a number of people who called to see if we were okay. They were Dawn, Brian, Susan, Shirley Duncan (called Thursday night and had more damage news than we had heard at that time), Marjie Phipps (from Illinois), Gordon, Mary Bush, Max, Bruce (he called twice), Cheryl, Vi Sanders (from Missouri), Arphena (from Kansas), Mike Wolf (from former A. G. Edwards), and Mary Hale.

Local friends who called were Don Quinn, Brenda Minor, Janie and Mel, Betty and Weldon Curtis.

Nathan sent us a text message, asking if we were okay. I replied that we were.

This was an F3 tornado, doing extensive damage to Mena. The warning sirens might have sounded more than four times, but they were blown out. It will take a long time for the cleanup to be completed. Mama and Papa Borders' house was badly damaged. I believe that it will have to come down. I took a picture of it. The old house on Janssen had roof damage. Mammaw's house is okay as is the yellow brick house on Reeves. How fortunate we were to have no more than three deaths and thirty injured. We were blessed at our house to be okay and have everything intact, except for the one large oak tree.

I stopped by Mama and Papa Borders house one day and got a piece of board the tornado did not blow away. Lee cut it in half, so I could give Cheryl a piece. Their house was torn down.

What a Christmas!

It was Tuesday, December 21, 2010, and I still had fifty-eleven things to do, which was why I went straight to the piano and began playing to my heart's content. The "yet-to-do" list kept floating through my mind, but I ignored it and relaxed with an excerpt from the third movement of Rachmaninoff's Second Concerto, which I had memorized some years earlier.

I enjoyed hearing the melody flow from my fingers until I saw a car in the driveway. Oh well, no matter. It was someone needing Lee to do a machinist job for them, and they will go to his shop located in our side yard. I continued playing but noticed that the car drove up to the house. They probably thought that Lee was in the house. I would just go to the door and tell them that Lee was in the shop. As I approached the door going onto the carport, I froze. I looked again to be sure that I was not mistaken. No, I was right, but what a surprise! There stood two of our grown grandsons, Neal and Nate.

Lee was already there talking to them. I rushed outside and hugged both of them. My! What a delight to have them here. We were laughing and talking as we entered the house. I asked them if their dad knew where they were. They said that they planned to surprise him when he arrived on Thursday. Almost before we had time to sit down, they asked about the Christmas lights attached to the front of the house. Lee told them that he and I had hung two strings of icicle lights on the front of the house but had not put the third section up yet. They immediately got up, went outside, and put the last string of lights in place. A little later, they went to town and returned with another set of lights, which they put up in maple tree in our front yard. I looked forward to the evening when we would turn on the lights and enjoy them.

Nate, knowing where I kept my jigsaw puzzles, got one out, and we began working on it along with playing cards and games. After a while, I prepared some supper for us and then it was dark enough to turn on the Christmas lights. What a delight to see them glowing, and the maple tree looked very dressed up.

We returned to our games until bedtime when I told them good night in a way I had done when they were little and would come for a visit, "Both of you dream of lollipops and sugar plum fairies."

For the most part, we spent the next day playing games, cards, working on the puzzle, and discussing ways they might surprise their dad when he arrived. However, I injected something else in our schedule. Lee and I had made a date with a local glass company to have the windows in our house replaced, so I recruited the boys to assist us in removing all of the drapes, curtains, and Venetian blinds from the windows. We also took down anything on the walls that were close to the windows to keep them from falling. However, we still managed to squeeze in several games.

Thursday was here. Brian sent me a text message about ten thirty, saying that he had a late start but was on his way.

I shared this information with the boys and said, "'You had better decide on your surprise plan now."

Nate replied, "I think I will hide the car now, so Dad won't see it when he arrives."

I called a neighbor, explained the situation, and asked if the boys could park the car at their house for a while.

The neighbor chuckled and replied, "Bring the car over any time. It can't be seen by Brian and there is plenty of room to park it."

Nate relocated the car, and we resumed our games. We received several messages from Brian, and the last one stated that he was driving through a small town ten miles away from us. I told the boys that it was time to put their surprise into action. They decided to hide in the living room, and as Brian came into the den from another door, they would slip out the front door, go get the car, and ease back to our house. We didn't have long to wait now.

We watched out the living room window and waited. Then suddenly, there was Brian driving up our driveway. The boys got in place, and I went outside to welcome him home. As we came into the den, I heard the front door open and close, but I kept talking as though nothing was going on. I almost blew the whole surprise, however, as I was talking to Brian about the new windows and directed his attention to the lovely new kitchen window. I was so happy about it because it was now one window instead of the two old ones that had been there since Lee built the house. It gave me a panoramic view, *but* it would have been a disaster if Brian had looked out the window and saw his two boys. In a few minutes, the carport door opened, and there stood Neal and Nate, grinning from ear to ear. Brian's face was simply glowing.

Amid hearty rounds of hugs and laughter, Brian looked at them and said, "This is the best Christmas present I could wish for."

Finally things calmed down, and we enjoyed the rest of the day. We played cards and games until quite late. Then everyone said good night (with lollipops and sugar plum fairies), and we retired for the night.

Friday morning was Christmas Eve. We all slept later than usual. Lee and I were the first to get up. As I prepared breakfast, Brian walked into the kitchen with Nate following a short time later. It was barely daylight when I saw a truck coming up our driveway.

I told Lee, "That looks like our neighbor. I wonder if they have a problem and need you to repair something?"

The neighbor got out of his truck and said, "I brought you something for Christmas"

At that time, Erinn, a granddaughter, popped out of their truck with a wide grin on her face. I just stood there and experienced great surprise for the second time in a matter of a few days.

The neighbor told us that "Erinn had driven from Seattle, Washington, and arrived at my garage a little while ago and asked if she could park her car here and surprise you. I told her that it would be fine, and she could park her car next to the car Neal and Nate had parked theirs. Then we waited for lights to come on in your house, so we would know that you folks were awake."

With laughter, hugs and hearty thanks to our neighbor, we went inside. I rushed to the bedroom where the boys were sleeping and woke them up with the good news of Erinn's arrival.

We spent part of the day playing more games and finishing the one thousand–piece puzzle and started another one. Then we loaded into our cab truck and took a long drive. A call from our oldest daughter, Dawn, saying she and her family would be here in a few hours took my thinking to preparing supper. Arriving home from the drive, I assigned duties to everyone, and by the time Dawn and family arrived, Christmas ham, candied sweet potatoes, creamed Irish potatoes (Lee loved to have those potatoes with every main meal), a broccoli and rice salad, cornbread, and of course, our traditional Christmas cake was ready. After the blessing, we dug right in until everyone was very full. After the dishes were washed, everyone gathered in the living room while I read the Christmas story from the Bible. Then we opened gifts and had a delightful time. We called Susan, our youngest daughter, and then returned to the game board. Again? Yep, and we enjoyed every minute. Before we knew it, time had passed so quickly and departure time was upon us. It was hard to say goodbye, but oh, my *what a Christmas*!

There's a Worm on the Loose in Church

Every other Tuesday and Friday, Joann and I would meet at the church to practice on a piano/organ duet for offertory for the next Sunday. On April 27, we met as usual to go over a piece of music. Joann did not have a book, so we went to the workroom to make copies. The copier would not print out a whole sheet of music. Either the top or bottom of the page would be cut off. Finally I went to Pam and asked her if she could help us. She changed some settings on the copier, and still, part of the music was missing. After a couple of tries, she got everything included on the copy.

Joann ran off copies of music while I used the paper cutter to trim the excess paper. After several minutes, she asked me if I had the music all trimmed up.

I replied, "No, I am looking for a worm."

Something had stung me on my neck. I reached up with my hand and slung it. Then I immediately looked on the floor, so I could dispose of it properly. There was nothing there. I searched farther and farther but found nothing. Joann began searching also. I looked through the wastepaper basket, behind boxes, on the cabinet top but found nothing. Joann asked me what I thought it was, and I said that it felt like a worm. It was soft and fuzzy. Just then, Bro. David came in the workroom and walked over to the worktable. He reached for an open box of crackers.

I said, "Uh, Bro. David, you may want to take a peek inside that box before you eat any of the crackers. You see, there is a worm on the loose around here somewhere."

He simply chuckled, picked up his box, and headed for the door while asking me what I was doing with a worm anyhow. Regretting that a worm was on the loose in church, Joann and I continued our search but with no luck.

Finally we gathered our music and went to the auditorium to practice. The duet was not real easy, but by the time we had gone over it a couple of times, we felt that we could have it ready by Sunday, and there was always Friday when we could go over it again. We finished our practice and went home.

The next morning, I went to the church to play for Susie Brumbelow's funeral. I needed to make a copy of a piece of music from one of my books. The copier did the same thing it did yesterday, it cut off some of the notes. After a couple of tries, I went and asked Lisa if she could help me. We went to the copy machine, and she showed me what to do make the copies turn out right.

As we were talking, I said, "Oh, by the way, keep your eyes out for a renegade worm that is on the loose in this room."

I told her what had happened yesterday, and she said, "If that had happened to me, I would have been screaming." At that moment, she exclaimed, "There it is!"

I looked where she was pointing, and sure enough, there was a small, fuzzy worm on the floor. Just at that time, Bro. David appeared in the workroom door.

He said, "What are you two up to?"

I replied, "Come over here, look. You see, there was a worm, and there he is." I asked if I could put it in the wastepaper basket or flush it down the commode.

Bro. David said the basket was fine.

I picked him up and plopped him in the wastepaper basket.

As I got my music and started toward the auditorium to play for the funeral, I thought, *Thank goodness, the case of the worm on the loose in church has been solved.*

Little House on the Prairie

It was another lovely day, mild temperatures and clear blue skies. On the spur of the moment, I decided to wash all the bedroom curtains. This was an easy task in itself because the washing machine does most of the work but then the thought occurred to me that the windowsills and Venetian blinds also needed a cleaning. How I wished that our blinds were the wide wooden kind, instead of the very narrow metal ones I was now staring at. Cleaning them was no simple task. They wiggle around as you wipe a damp cloth across a slat, and the section you are trying to clean will quickly flop down, slipping from your grasp. Then of course, you run your finger across a slat to be sure that you are not cleaning one you have just done. It was a time-consuming project. Thankfully just about then, the wash cycle was completed. I took my time hanging out the curtains in the bright sunshine and did not hurry to get back to my cleaning job.

Sometime after lunch, dark clouds began to roll in, so I rushed out to the clothesline and hurriedly began tossing the curtains into the laundry basket just as light rain began to fall.

By the time I took the last one off the line, I thought, *These are already nicely sprinkled, so I will iron them immediately and hang them back up on the curtain rods.*

After I got in the house, I set up the ironing board, plugged in the iron, and got the spray starch from the utility closet for the light-weight cotton curtains. They have ruffles, and a little stiffness makes them hang better. It was time for my favorite TV program, so I could enjoy watching it while I ironed.

As I began ironing, I smelled an unusual fragrance. In fact, it became almost overpowering. After a short time, the bottom of my iron turned dark, and the ironing board cover changed to a reddish color, and both reeked with the fragrance. I was engrossed in the TV program I was watching, so I gave the smell a fleeting thought and kept on ironing. I had ironed six of the eight curtain panels; four of them were quite ruffled and had two matching valances. By now, my attention was completely focused on the aroma, which had filled the entire house. I went around opening windows in every room and turned on the ceiling fans to high speed. I examined the curtains I had already hung up and noticed with great relief that they seemed to be okay. I went to the utility closet to get another can and returned to the ironing board. I changed my method of ironing with the remaining two panels. You see, what I *had* been using was "Pledge!"

A few days later, I was ironing again. When I made that first stroke of the iron on a pair of slacks, I knew immediately that something would have to be done. The heat of the iron on the ironing board cover brought back *that* fragrance. This time, I was ironing clothes that we would wear, and we simply could not go around spreading that aroma everywhere we went.

I thought of buying a new cover, but that would mean another trip to town in one day, and besides, I needed to get those clothes ironed now. I thought for a moment about what I might do. Then I went to the rag bag. There I found a discarded sheet. I folded it over several times and placed it on top of the strongly scented ironing board cover. I put the pair of slacks back on the ironing board and applied the iron. Perfect. There was no fragrance. I continued ironing all the other pieces. It didn't matter; I could pin the sheet down tight later. For now, I had taken care of the fragrance problem, and vowed that from now on, I would pay closer attention to what can I took from the utility closet.

October 16, 2010

Prayer Time

One evening, I was playing solitaire when my cell phone rang. It was a friend of mine calling to ask for prayers for another friend, who had suffered a heart attack and had just been taken to the hospital. I assured the caller that I would spend time in prayer for our friend. We hung up, and I began to pray. Then I stopped.

I said, "Lord, there are so many different thoughts going through my mind right now that I am having difficulty concentrating on my friend. Would you please remove all of the distracting thoughts and give me a clear mind for this prayer concern?"

Immediately there came to my mind a beautiful green country hillside with a narrow dirt path and flowers on one side on the path. They were so fresh looking and in colors of yellow, pink, and deep purple. I was standing in the path, then suddenly, Jesus was standing beside me. If I had used a whole bottle of bleach on a new white sheet, I could not have made it as white as Jesus' robe. It did not sparkle or glow, but it was the most brilliant white I had ever seen. Jesus turned his head toward me, and He was smiling. His face showed gentleness, kindness, and caring. His eyes had such a warmth and loving look.

He spoke to me, saying, "Linda, I am here."

At that moment, the scene disappeared. I didn't move for several moments, letting what I had just experienced soak in. I thanked Jesus for that experience and resumed praying for my friend with total concentration. Again, I thanked Jesus for the scene He had put in my mind and then cleared my mind to pray. I often recall that time with joy and thanksgiving. My friend? That person recovered and is doing well.

Pain and Agony

I answered the ringing phone. The lady calling identified herself as the publishing editor of a new magazine soon to start publication. She wanted me to write an article for the first issue.

I said, "I am sure you have the wrong number."

She replied, "No, I am certain I have the right person. I have read a few of your stories in a magazine, and I think you would add much interest for our readers."

I thought to myself that this was a most unusual conversation. How was I going to convince this lady that I was not the person she needed? I asked her some questions about this new magazine, and all though she answered my questions, I did not learn a lot. I was wracking my brain for a way to convince her that I simply was not the person she was looking for. She was very polite but determined that I be the one to prepare the material she desired for the magazine.

I had exhausted all of my ways of declining to write the article, and besides, I needed to get supper started. I told her once again that I was sure I was not the person she needed when a new idea occurred to me. That would surely give me a way out.

I asked her, "What is the name of the new magazine?"

She replied in a quivering voice, "*Pain and Agony.*"

It was at that moment that I recognized the voice of the caller. It was my granddaughter, Laura. We both had a hearty laugh over the trick she had enjoyed playing on me.

Several days later, Susan, my daughter and Laura's mother, called me.

She asked, "Would you like to return the favor and play a trick on Laura?"

I replied, "Just tell me what I need to do."

She explained the situation to me as follows, "Laura was leaving her apartment very early one morning to go to work. The entire neighborhood was still sleeping peacefully. Laura had barely backed out of her driveway when her car alarm went off, sounding like a tornado warning siren. She had bought a used Mercedes Benz a couple of months earlier and was unaware that it had an alarm system. She pushed every button she could find, but the shrill sound continued. By now, people in their sleepwear were at their windows, hollering for her to turn the noisy thing off. Laura was frantic and continued pushing buttons, hoping one of them would silence the blaring sound that had now awakened the entire neighborhood, but the sound kept on as Laura drove block after block.

"Finally she arrived at a gas station, and immediately a serviceman appeared. She hollered the obvious problem, and he told her that he was not familiar with Mercedes Benz. She drove down the highway with the blaring alarm, waking everybody up along the way. She felt somewhat like Paul Revere as he went through the countryside, hollering, 'The British are coming!' Finally she arrived at a Mercedes Benz shop, and they cut the wire, which brought blissful silence. The man said the alarm was faulty and would have to be replaced. She went on to work pondering if she even wanted an alarm system installed."

Well, I saw a golden opportunity. I called Laura.

Using a deep Southern accent, I said, "Am I speaking to Miss Laura Warren?"

She replied that she was Laura Warren and asked who I was.

Keeping my accent, I gave a fictitious name and explained that I was calling from the main office of Mercedes Benz and had received a report of a problem with her car. Continuing I said, "Now, Miss Warren, we want you to be happy with your car, and we want your neighbors to continue liking you also. We have a replacement part we will be happy to send to you. Any Mercedes Benz shop can install it for you. When you receive your new part, just call one of the shops and make an appointment. The replacement part is available at a mere cost of 559 dollars and ninety-five cents, plus shipping and handling, of course. We can get this part off to you today. All we need is your credit card number and current address."

Total silence followed then Laura exclaimed, "*Grandma*! That's you. Boy, you really had me going there for a few minutes."

I asked, "Would this story do for the first issue of your new magazine, *Pain and Agony*?"

We both laughed until we were out of breath and have referred to it at times since then.

At a later date, Susan and Laura were here visiting. They made an appointment for a hairdo at the beauty shop where Cindy, a friend of Susan's since their school days.

After they had their hair all fixed up, Laura said to Susan, "Let's call Grandma and play a trick on her."

Cindy overheard their conversation, and as the two were walking toward the phone, Cindy asked, "What are you going to do?"

Laura replied their intent, and Cindy said, "That is a terrible thing to do."

Susan and Laura laughed and said they did it all the time and that I thought it was funny. That mattered not one bit to Cindy. She stated clearly and firmly that they would play no tricks using her phone. Susan and Laura had to go someplace else to have their fun.

That Frame!

During the spring of 2020, I decided to tackle a project I had been thinking about for a very long time. The fence row that ran along the north side of the property line had, over many years, become very overgrown with briers, sticker vines, wild plants, and numerous other growths. It was extremely dense, *sooo* early one morning, I gathered the garden hoe and a pair of hand clippers, my cell phone, and went to work. There were trees along the fence row that had lower limbs that were in my way. I worked a week or so, trimming where I could. I laid the clippers on an old metal frame lying on the ground nearby while I gathered up the clippings.

After making a good sized pile, I reached for the clippers, but they were not there. The frame was clearly visible with nothing to obstruct my view. Those clippers just were not there. I searched everywhere I had been working, thinking that perhaps I was mistaken as to where I had placed them. A very thorough search resulted in no clippers. I gave up and went to the house.

Later that afternoon, I returned to the fence row feeling sure that I would quickly see those clippers. After a lengthy search, I stood there quite puzzled as to where in the world I had put them. I thought back over that morning. I had not gone anywhere else during the time I was working, so they had to be there somewhere. But where! Again, I walked back to the house with no clippers in hand. That evening, I made another long search along the fence row with no success. I repeated my search around the frame, but there were no clippers there. Disappointed, I went to the house.

The next morning, feeling optimistic, I went to search again, thinking that it was a new day, I was rested, and I would find those clippers. Yeah. Well, that balloon was popped quickly as that search ended like the others—no clippers. I wondered if some neighborhood dog or woods animal had carried them off. I was not getting any clearing done this way, so I decided that I would go to the hardware store and buy a pair or clippers.

I got ready and started to town. On the way, I had a thought that took my mind back a number of years. Lee, my husband, worked for the post office and had to attend a meeting in Little Rock. He asked me to go with him, and I could shop while he was in the meeting. I agreed and off we went. I let him out at the meeting place and drove the short distance to a mall. Later that afternoon, when the meeting was over and I picked Lee up, he said that he needed to go to Sears, so we went to that same mall. While he was looking for what he wanted, I just browsed around. Then I saw an item which caught my attention. There in front of me was a row of saws. Now we have several saws at home, but these saws in Sears were assorted sizes, from large to small. I stood there and thought of the many times I had wished for a small saw that would be easier for me to handle, and there was just the size I wanted. Just at that time, Lee walked up and said he was ready to go.

I showed the little saw to him and said, "I would like to get this little saw."

Lee replied, "Mama, anything you want sawed off I will do it."

We left the store, but I felt a little disappointed to leave the saw behind.

On my way to town, I kept thinking about that saw, so when I entered the hardware store, a clerk asked if he could help me. I told him that I needed a pair of hand clippers.

He smiled and said, "They are right over here on the next row."

He showed me the different kinds they had, and I saw one like my lost one, so he took it off the hook and asked if there was anything else he could help me with.

I replied, "Do you have any small saws?"

He nodded and led me to where they were on display. Oh! There was a saw exactly like the one I had seen at Sears in Little Rock.

I excitedly exclaimed, "Yes, that one is what I am looking for."

I could hardly believe that I had found that saw. I made my purchase and quickly (not breaking the speed limit) drove home. I immediately changed my clothes, and with new clippers and that special saw in hand, I headed for the fence row.

As I approached, I jerked to a sudden stop and stared. There on the frame lay my lost clippers. I just stood there for several minutes and looked at them. They were in the exact spot where I remembered placing them. After I got over the shock, I had a delightful time sawing off limbs and branches. From time to time, I looked over at the frame, and sure enough, those previously lost clippers were still there. I made five high piles of what I had sawed off. Dawn came over for a visit and finished the last several feet. We piled the limbs, twigs, branches, and vines altogether. As we finished the project, I looked at the fence row and smiled. Not only had I achieved my goal for clearing the fence row, but I had recovered the lost clippers *and* purchased the saw that I had wanted years ago.

I called Katie, a good friend, and told her my experience, and she said, "Linda, I believe that because you honored your husband and didn't go ahead and buy that saw at Sears, that the Lord knew that you wanted that little saw, so He blinded your eyes to not see the clippers. So you bought a new pair and got that little saw."

I believe that God was in charge of the situation also and perhaps smiled when He saw me sawing away at those limbs and branches. I did say a prayer of thanks.

Later I called the church and asked if they could send someone out to haul off the piles I had made. They said yes, and a few days later, a young man came out and cleared the spot of all the piles. Job done.

Ripples and Waves

I was cleaning house when I realized that I needed a brush with stiffer bristles. I keep a box of brushes with different strength bristles in the washhouse. Now the washhouse is the storage room at the head of the carport. The reason it is called the washhouse is because when Lee my husband built our house that he forgot to allow a place for the washer and dryer, so they were placed in the storage room.

I stepped out on the carport and stopped in my tracks. I thought, *What in the world is that sound?*

I stood there and listened. It seemed to be coming from the shed, another storage place. I started walking that way then running. Oh, no! The tall piped water faucet was pouring forth water like a gusher. I could go wading in the standing water, but there were also ripples and waves of the water rushing in different directions. I hurried over to the faucet, and amid the squirting and splashing of water in my face and wearing wet clothes, I attempted to turn the faucet off. I got in every position humanly possible and exerted every ounce of strength I possessed to absolutely *no* avail. I tried over and over again without moving that thing the slightest bit of an inch.

Standing there with water running off of me, I looked heavenward and said, "Lord, what do I do now?"

If I had thought for another second, I would have realized that I could call the church, where I am a member, and they would have gladly sent a couple of men to resolve the problem, but at that instant, my cell phone, which I had placed in a dry spot, rang. Breathlessly I answered. It was my son, Brian, who lives seven hours away.

He asked, "What are you doing?"

I explained the whole wet situation.

He asked, "Do you want me to come and fix it?"

I gave a puny chuckle and replied, "Yes, why don't you just drop over and take care of this problem."

He said, "Mamma, I will be there in about ten minutes."

I gasped and excitingly exclaimed, "What!"

He said, "I planned a surprise visit. I just passed through town."

We said our goodbyes, and I stood there amazed that God had a solution to my problem and a delightful visit with Brian also. He did arrive in a short time, stopped his truck, jumped out, and ran over to the still-gushing faucet. I watched from a distance where the spray couldn't reach me and joyfully saw that gush of water become smaller and smaller till there was not even an occasional drip coming out of that faucet.

I said, "'Thank you, God." Then I gave Brian a dual hug, one for being home and for stopping that river of water.

I looked at that dripless faucet with tremendous delight and pleasure.

Putting First Things First

For several weeks, I had been searching for a list of the moves we made when Lee was working for the Kansas City Southern Railroad. He was a part of the Signal Corp, and the work they did usually took two to three weeks to get done. Then they were sent to another town to do another job. I kept a record of the fifty-four moves we made in seven years, from 1955 to 1962.

That was fifty-nine years ago. Fast forward to year 2021. As I was doing my search, I saw a small rubber doll that Lee and I had bought for Dawn when she was four months. The doll had detachable arms, legs, and head.

While living in Shreveport in a trailer park, one day as Dawn was playing outside our trailer, I noticed that one leg was gone. I searched the whole area around the trailer but did not find the leg. The next day, Lee came home from work and said that the Signal Corp was moving to another job, which meant that we were moving also. Along with getting things ready for travel, I made another search for that doll leg but with no success. The next day, we were on our way. The Corp was on the new job for six weeks, which was unusual, and then we were sent back to Shreveport.

Being familiar with the trailer park we had lived in before, we returned to that same one and got assigned to the very same trailer lot as before. Several of the people we had met earlier were still living there, which was so nice to already be acquainted. The next day after we moved in, Dawn was playing in our tiny yard. I went outside to be with her, and as I was looking around, I saw something over in the tall grass.

As I got nearer, I exclaimed, "Oh, my word!"

There was *that* doll's leg. Perfectly intact, no cuts or broken places. I picked it up to examine it closer. It was the right size, correct leg, and looked to be made the same way as the attached leg. I got Dawn and rushed into the trailer. Getting the doll, I positioned the leg, and it popped right in place. I stood there amazed that we were sent back to Shreveport, went to the previous trailer park we had lived in, and got the same trailer space. And besides, the doll leg had not been thrown away, cut up by the yardman's lawn mower, or picked up by some other child. I took the doll to the bathroom and gave that leg a good scrubbing and disinfected it. Wow! It looked just like the other leg.

When Lee returned home from work later that day, I showed him the doll and told him what had happened. He was as surprised as I had been and agreed that the doll leg looked as though it had been on the doll all the time. That doll still looks nearly new and with two good legs.

In looking for that list of moves, I undertook the tremendous task of going through many boxes and folders and searching through closets, file cabinets, and drawers. I had stacks and piles everywhere.

It would be midmorning, and this thought would come to mind, *Linda, devotional time.*

I thought that I would do it after lunch, but after lunch, I would be bogged down in those stacks and piles and thought I would take time after supper to do my Bible reading, but by that time, I was so tired that I just didn't do it then either. This went on for weeks with that gentle nudge coming into my mind regularly, but I kept thinking I would find that list soon and get back on the daily time of Bible reading.

Then one evening, I said to myself, "This has got to stop. I need and want to get back to my time in reading the Bible."

The next morning after breakfast, I started toward a stack of papers and stopped. Instead, I picked up a copy of *Jesus Calling*. I read the thought for that day then looked up the scriptures listed there. Afterward, I had a time of prayer ending with asking God to please show me where that list of railroad moves was. I had asked

Him before, but that was during the time that I had put Him aside to go through the mountains of items I had to look at.

About fifteen minutes later, I went to one of the bedrooms and looked in a box. There was a folder against one side of the box marked, "Railroad Moves"! I jerked the folder out of the box, eagerly opened it, and there was the long-lost list. I stood there staring at it. I had taken everything out of that box earlier but just did not see that folder up next to the side of the box. I stood there staring at the list.

Smiling, I thanked the Lord for leading me to the right spot and reminded myself that I must always start each day with my heavenly Father and *put first things first*.

Treasure in the Woods

In my wooded area next to the side yard, the trees and under-growth were very dense. I had worked countless times with a hand-saw and a pair of clippers to thin out some of the brush, but the job required bigger equipment and more power, so having spent several hours trimming and making piles of brush, I decided to get some-one that could make more progress in a quicker time. I called Larry, a neighbor from past years, and explained what I wanted and if he could do the job. He replied that he could and would come over the next day.

The next morning, I walked into the woods and scooped up the piles of brush I had made the day before and made one big pile that Larry could pick up with his tractor bucket.

Larry arrived on schedule, and we walked to the woods to discuss what I wanted. Because of the density, it was difficult to maneuver the tractor. As I was returning to the house, I heard crackling sounds as trees were being uprooted and crashing down to the ground. I smiled in anticipation of how nice and neat the woods would look when he finished.

It took a number of days for Larry to get just one area thinned out and haul the uprooted trees to a place in the open back field to be burned. There were still places where I could use my clippers, so early one morning, before Larry came, I entered my woods and started clipping and making a pile of trimmings. After a while, I saw Larry drive up and start unloading his tractor. I quickly gathered up my last bit of clippings, and after a brief visit, I went to the house. Larry worked for hours in one spot that was like a jungle. He kept working back and forth, and finally, I could see a very welcomed thinning among the trees that were left standing. I continued working in the house as the day passed on to late afternoon.

There was a knock at the door. I had not heard anyone drive up, so I wondered who it was. Opening the door, I saw Larry standing there.

I asked, "Do you need something?"

He held a hand out and asked, "Are these your glasses?"

I immediately recognized them as the pair of new prescription glasses I had received only a few weeks ago. I reached out my hand to take them and told Larry that yes, they were mine and explained that I had been clipping branches and twigs just that morning.

He said, "You know, it is a true miracle that I didn't crush them into tiny pieces because I have worked in that same spot for hours, running the tractor back and forth, then driving the tractor bucket across the ground to pick up debris."

The glasses were in perfect shape with not even one tiny scratch anywhere. When I had gone to the woods early that morning, I was wearing my glasses, but after a while, I took them off and tucked one stem into the top of my shirt. Somewhere along the way, they slipped out, and I had not noticed. I agreed with Larry that it was a miracle that with all the times the tractor had been driven over and over the same ground, they were not a small pile of broken, crushed pieces. I took a look out to the woods and smiled. I told Larry that the spot where he had been working looked so thinned out and clean. From then on, I either kept those glasses on or left them in the house!

Looking Ahead

In thinking back over all the wonderful, sometimes trying, memories I have experienced, I ponder the possibility of having a complete family gathering. It would be quite an undertaking. I imagine such a time as being like all the other times when some of us have been together. There would be much laughter, good-natured teasing, playing games, gathering around the piano to harmonize singing hymns, and favorite foods to enjoy. We would delight in watching Naomi, Evelyn, Lucy, Sydney, and Lydia as they played with Aubree and Jacob, being older, entertaining themselves. Parents, Nate, Mandy, Abigail, Ryan, and Caleb, enjoyed seeing the cousins playing together. Looking ahead, this would be great fun and quite an adventure.

Lollipops and Sugarplum Fairies

It was always a delight when any of the children and grandchildren came home for a visit. The time went so quickly as we had fun playing games, reading stories, and catching up on what they had been doing. Sometimes it seemed to me that the grandchildren felt a little uneasy not to be sleeping in their own bed. As they would change into their pajamas and brush their teeth, I thought about how I could make them feel more relaxed to get into a different bed. I tried putting a chocolate mint on each pillow, and even though they squealed with delight, it did not seem to relieve their mood. Suddenly I recalled an expression I had heard many times during my childhood.

I gathered them around me and said, "Now I want you to listen to what I am going to say. I am asking you to do a favor for me, and you can do it right there in bed. Okay, jump in bed and cover up real good. Here we go. I want you to close your eyes and, oops, wait a minute. I said e-y-e-s, that means both eyes. Close them tight. Now I want you to think of yummy lollipops and dainty, colorful sugarplum fairies. You can design the lovely costume for the sugarplum fairies in any color you want, maybe your favorite color or a color you see in this room. Think about it for several minutes. Now then, you have had time to look around the room to see the colors, so I am going to tell you good night and turn the light off. Now you can get busy thinking about those sugarplum fairies."

After I gave each one a hug, I flipped the light switch and quietly left them to their thinking.

The grandchildren grew from early childhood to the kindergarten and grade school years. With each visit to our house, I continued to use the bedtime phrase, "Dream about lollipops and sugarplum fairies." They always gave me a wide smile with a nod of their head and went to bed. Before I knew it, they were in high school. My goodness, where did the time go? Well, I figured that they probably felt like they were too grown up to hear that longtime bedtime phrase now, but when one of them came for a visit (Oh, my, he was driving his own car now), we had supper and a good chat; he announced that he was tired and was going to bed. We said good night, and he started down the hall. He stopped, turned around, and looked at me. I asked him if he wanted anything. He grinned and nodded his head.

I thought for a moment and then grinning, I said, "Now you be sure and dream about lollipops and sugarplum fairies."

His smile became wider as he replied, "Now I can go to bed."

More years passed and now those grandchildren were in their twenties and thirties. They didn't get to our house very often for a visit now. The lollipops and sugarplum fairies sort of slipped to the back of my mind, even though when any of them did come to see us, they always waited for me to send them off to bed with that old familiar phrase.

Last Thanksgiving, there were fifteen family members here at our house. What a grand time we had; laughter was ringing through the house. We gathered around the table with a card table added at one end. We joined hands, the blessing was said, and we filled our plates (more than once). After we finally ate our fill, we cleared the table, washed the dishes, and got the kitchen in order. Our capacity for food had certainly been filled, so now all we wanted to do was sit down and try to get a deep breath.

We began reminiscing and teasing each other. A grandson, Caleb, walked over to me, and with a twinkle in his eyes, he handed me a lovely, wrapped box from him and his sister, Abigail. I was totally surprised and could not imagine what that box contained. Quickly I removed the beautiful bow and wrapping paper. Down in the tissue paper was an object that I hastily took out and in my hand was a small dainty sugarplum fairy complete with a very charming costume. I saw a bit of color among the tissue paper, so I looked further and brought out a handful of lollipops. Memories flooded my mind of past years, and it touched my heart that they remembered the times I had said, "Now you dream about lollipops and sugarplum fairies."

Those Special Grandchildren
and Great-Grandchildren

There are those things that they do making for very sweet memories. I have some lovely pieces of pottery that Laura made and gave to me. Somehow a cup of hot tea tastes more flavorful in one of her pottery cups. I like to have the bowls sitting around, so I can enjoy seeing them. I love to work jigsaw puzzles with grandson Nate.

One day, I received a package from Erinn. Opening it, I stood there with a look of total surprise on my face. She had sent me a puzzle of Hotel Queen Wilhilmena, a lovely lodge atop the second tallest mountain in Arkansas. It is a delight to put together.

I remember one Christmastime Neal and Nathan arrived at our house. I had not had time to put up the outside lights, so they quickly got all the lights together, brought a ladder to the house, and in no time, we had twinkling lights. They looked so bright and festive as any of us drove up the driveway to our house. The sugarplum fairy and lollipops from Caleb and Abigail bring back very special memories. It had been a long, long time since I had enjoyed a lollipop. Jacob, Aubree, Evelyn, Naomi, Lucy, Sydney, and Lydia made up the rest of the group. I have received drawings, pictures, and paper flowers from some of the group. Each one is so special. What fun it is to play chase, read to them, and just watch as they play.

About the Author

She was born Linda MeLee Borders in Houston, Texas, but grew up in Mena, Arkansas. She had a very happy childhood. In addition to her parents, she had grandparents, great-grandparents, aunts, uncles, cousins, and childhood friends who made her growing-up experiences even richer. During the summer before her senior year in high school, she met Lee Gandy, a young man who along with about forty-five other young men made up the Signal Corp of the Kansas City Southern Railroad. They had been sent to Mena to do a job that was expected to take several months. During that time, they began dating, but for the first seven weeks, their dates were at Linda's home, giving her parents a little time to get better acquainted with Lee. They were married the next May. Besides adjusting to married life, she began to feel like a traveling salesperson. It normally took the Signal Corp a couple of weeks to get their job done unless they had special work to do. Well, they moved fifty-four times in seven years, anywhere from Kansas City to New Orleans and countless places in between. Their three wonderful children—Dawn, Brian, and Susan—came along. When Dawn started in first grade, the other children and Linda went to Mena while Lee continued working on KCS and went home on the weekends.

After the children grew up and left home, Linda attended college and got a degree in elementary education and taught fourth grade for several years. Time passed and they were blessed with six grandchildren. After sixty-three years of marriage, Lee passed away. There are now eight great-grandchildren, each one a complete delight. Linda is still a church organist for which she is grateful. It gives her great joy. She looks back over the years and sees God's ever-present hand in her life. For this, she is also grateful.

A note from the author

What an Adventure! This book is full of true occurrences my family and I experienced with the exception of two of the stories: "The Friendship Bowl" and "A Country Christmas." It is true that I have the friendship bowl and that my great-grandmother received it from her neighbor who had moved to the United States from Austria. The story "A Country Christmas" was told to me by a friend Lucy Ryals Lawshee, and I wrote it in story form keeping all her facts accurate.

Most of all, I want to give thanks to God for His loving watch care and the many blessings He has placed in my life, seeing me safely through all these experiences.

Printed in the USA
CPSIA information can be obtained
at www.ICGtesting.com
LVHW041311021123
762340LV00001B/81